Dictionary
of Magic

MIDCENTURY
REFERENCE LIBRARY

DAGOBERT D. RUNES, Ph.D., General Editor

AVAILABLE

Beethoven Encyclopedia
Dictionary of American Grammar
  and Usage
Dictionary of American Maxims
Dictionary of American Proverbs
Dictionary of Ancient History
Dictionary of Arts and Crafts
Dictionary of the Arts
Dictionary of Civics and Government
Dictionary of European History
Dictionary of Etiquette
Dictionary of Foreign Words
  and Phrases
Dictionary of Early English
Dictionary of Last Words
Dictionary of Latin Literature
Dictionary of Linguistics
Dictionary of Mysticism
Dictionary of Mythology
Dictionary of Pastoral Psychology
Dictionary of Philosophy
Dictionary of Psychoanalysis
Dictionary of Science and Technology

Dictionary of Sociology
Dictionary of Word Origins
Dictionary of World Literature
Encyclopedia of Aberrations
Encyclopedia of the Arts
Encyclopedia of Atomic Energy
Encyclopedia of Criminology
Encyclopedia of Literature
Encyclopedia of Psychology
Encyclopedia of Religion
Encyclopedia of Substitutes and
  Synthetics
Encyclopedia of Vocational Guidance
Illustrated Technical Dictionary
Labor Dictionary
Liberal Arts Dictionary
Military and Naval Dictionary
New Dictionary of American History
New Dictionary of Psychology
Protestant Dictionary
Slavonic Encyclopedia
Theatre Dictionary
Tobacco Dictionary

FORTHCOMING

Buddhist Dictionary
Dictionary of American Folklore
Dictionary of the American Indian
Dictionary of the American Language
Dictionary of American Literature
Dictionary of American Men and Places
Dictionary of American Names
Dictionary of American Superstitions
Dictionary of American Synonyms
Dictionary of Anthropology
Dictionary of Astronomy
Dictionary of Dietetics
Dictionary of Discoveries and Inventions
Dictionary of Earth Sciences
Dictionary of Explorations
Dictionary of French Literature
Dictionary of Geography

Dictionary of German Literature
Dictionary of Hebrew Literature
Dictionary of Law
Dictionary of Magic
Dictionary of Mechanics
Dictionary of New Words
Dictionary of Poetics
Dictionary of the Renaissance
Dictionary of Russian Literature
Dictionary of Science
Dictionary of Social Science
Dictionary of Spanish Literature
Encyclopedia of Morals
Personnel Dictionary
Teachers' Dictionary
Writers' Dictionary

PHILOSOPHICAL LIBRARY, INC.
Publishers

15 E. 40th Street

New York 16, N. Y.

Dictionary of Magic

Harry E. Wedeck

Lecturer in Classics
Brooklyn College, New York

Philosophical Library

New York

Printed in the United States of America

Introduction

What is magic? Have the weird or baneful phenomena associated with wizardry an independent existence and validity of their own? That magic has such an existence and a verifiable validity, is the traditional attitude of the mediaeval demonographers such as Martin Delrio, Father Guaccius, Sprenger and Kramer, the authors of the Malleus Maleficarum, along with a numberless host of actual practitioners in the occult arts, savants and princelings, kings and prelates.

It is also the view of many contemporary authorities, among them G. B. Gardner, A. E. Waite, J. J. Williams, Lewis Spence, and Montague Summers. To these investigators and historians, all manifestations of witchcraft, despite their inherent characteristics of functioning in opposition to the accepted and normally observed laws of nature, are palpable, demonstrable, and identifiable in their essential and distinctive features.

Another view maintains that all these demoniac or occult practices are merely imaginative, conceptual figments whose reality exists only in a fictional form or in the amorphous drifting legends of primitive folklore. If magic is real, and if it is capable of exerting influence on human beings and human situations, what is its significance? And what has been that significance throughout human history?

Magic, thaumaturgy, goety, in all its variousness and emphasis, since the very dawn of primal history, down through the tenebrous middle centuries, down to the present chaotic times, has always exerted a powerful appeal—to the earthy peasant and the old beldames of the tribe, to inquisitive scholars and scribes, and, notably, to the professional priest-magician, whose function was to apply the occult secrets to the spiritual governance of his people.

Magic was atmospheric, all pervasive, penetrating all phases of life, conditioning every human activity.

All continents have their magic motifs, their arcane secrets, their esoteric books and grimoires, their Keys of Solomon and the lore of Albertus Magnus, the accumulated Kabalistic knowledge transmitted by generations of adepts, wandering thaumaturgists, and learned seers. Some nations have guarded these secrets scrupulously. In some instances the secret knowledge has spread, through the basic folk-lore of tribal communities, into strange channels, mingling with streams of religious practices, absorbed by philo-sophic doctrines, built up into exclusive systems intended only for the rare adept.

Magic has been protean in form. It changes and remains the same in essential substance. It borrows from religion and the sciences, from literature and history, from medi-cine and from the unwritten folk codes. It is literate on occasion and it can also sink into barbarous formlessness, inarticulate, incomprehensible even to its practitioners. It extends from innocuous techniques, bordering on herbal lore and intended to cure simple ailments, down to awe-some performances of levitation, to the conjuration of maleficent demons who work woe upon the living enemy: to necromantic arts and divination that lead to converse with the dread but obedient spirits of the dead. All such manifestations and rituals belong to that strange art or skill that, by means of certain prescribed rites, at times by mysterious incantations and invocations, sometimes by still more malefic devices, seems to transcend natural fron-tiers and to exceed the normal potentialities of man.

In its essence, the sphere of magic, with all its obfuscating or sinister operations, rites, techniques, is a world of escape from the rigid sameness of this material cosmos that we know. The world of magic has its own laws, its own logic. Things happen therein because they are impossible. Noth-ing in this amazing yet dangerous region ever remains the same or palpable. Things fade and crumble into dust at a word. A wave of a potent wand creates magnificence. Men startlingly shrink in size, or change into wild animals: while mysterious elemental creatures, invisible and impalpable, are ubiquitously scouring the earth. Above all, the word, the sacred logos—embedded in the mystic Tetragrammaton, in the equally mystic Kabalistic permutations and combinations of letters and numbers, in the efficacious Key of Solomon—possesses the most dominant, the most infinite potency. Thought moves mountains, and the mind exults in its masterful supremacy.

It is, in another and related sense, the fairy tale become real. The eerie tales of childhood, that inspired dread or bewilderment, become, on a spacious, mature basis, logical and rational in their distorted, fantastic reality, while all that is stable and secure in the prosaic world is subject, at any impulsive moment, to occult mutabilities.

All these fantasies, these darksome procedures, these necromantic incantations and demoniac conjurations, these spells and the entire horrendous apparatus of magic: the furtive witches' Sabbat, the talismans inscribed with potent symbols, the circles and pentacles, the Black Mass, the perverted, blasphemous obscenities, would, in their cumulative import, remain a more or less innocuous phenomenon in the totality of human experience. They would be a phase of human crudity, or human whimsicality, matter for ridicule, or curiosity, or academic interest.

But witchcraft stepped beyond the frontiers of mere ritual, of conceptual fields. It entered into the palpable area of cosmic, human reality. And it was then that it became a menace, a cataclysm, and a tragedy. For witchcraft was never content with a mere ideology, with notions that had no physical reference. It extended into tangential fields, creating impacts on large masses of society, intruding into the social and political frame, and engendering disturbances that were disastrous in their effects. Magic, leaving its mystic home, stepped down into the earthy arena, bringing in its wake agonies and massacre. And witchcraft, in all these encounters, was invariably one of its own victims.

Although witchcraft, woven into the very living fibre, was a matter of wide and common practice among the Accadians and the Chaldeans, the Babylonians and Egyptians, the Greeks and the Romans, the sheer cumulative effect of the prevalence of diviners and warlocks, enchanters and necromancers reached such heights, in the course of the ages, and was so overwhelming, so disastrous in many instances, on the people, that formal laws and restrictive measures were established by king and emperor, senate and magistrate to abolish all such magical operations. Yet, with all the prohibitions, involving penalties of fines and banishment, torture and death, the practice, like some evil phoenix, rose from the dead ashes of seemingly final condemnation, and once again returned to its sinister operations.

The illustrations and instances that have been furnished are not exhaustive, but they demonstrably indicate that witchcraft was no mere phantasmal unsubstantiality, like Quixote's windmills. It was a palpable force, to be grappled with. It could be assailed by legal measures. Its practitioners and devotees could be arraigned and convicted, punished and massacred. It was, in short—or its manifestations were, which amounts to the same thing—an actuality that, in its tortuous assaults upon the individual, or upon masses of people, or even upon the state itself, tended toward slow but persistent undermining of the commonweal, both secular and spiritual. And, since the opposition between the two was diametrically at variance one with the other, the weaker contender was crushed. Yet—and this fact strikes an ominous note—the resilience of witchcraft is no rare symptom of these contemporary times. The occult arts never rest, never accept an ultimate defeat. They seep through the social structure, gathering new adherents, practicing mystic rituals in secret, consummating Satanic rites, and perpetuating, in an appreciable degree, the Chaldean priest-magicians, the mediaeval necromancers, and the mantic diviners.

H. E. W.

Dictionary
of Magic

A

Aaron's rod: A magic wand, adorned with an entwined serpent. When cast by Aaron before Pharaoh, it became a serpent. It is the symbol of the magician's efficacy.

Aba-aner: An ancient Egyptian magician.

Abaddon: A powerful demon.

Abaris: A Scythian magician, owner of a golden arrow by means of which he practiced transvection through the air. He was believed to be the master of the Greek philosopher Pythagoras.

Abigor: A monstrous demon.

Abracadabra: A magic formula used in incantations against sickness or ill luck. Usually the inscription appears on an amulet, in the form of an inverted pyramid: so that the first line reads:

ABRACADABRA

Each succeeding line is diminished by one letter, the last line reading:

A

The disease or ill fortune disappears as the magic formula itself dwindles away. The first mention of this term appears in the works of Quintus Severus Sammondicus, a physician of the third century A.D.

A similar formula, a Hebraic spell against the demon Shabriri, runs:

Shabriri
Briri
Riri
Iri
Ri

The demon shrinks with the decrease in the size of his name. Another instance is Ochnotinos, a demon who causes fever, which disappears with the diminution of his name, thus:

Ochnotinos

Chnotinos

Notinos

Tinos

Inos

Nos

Os

Abraxas: Among the Gnostics, a divine name, embodying magic significance.

Abraxas gems: Amulets used to ward off witchcraft.

Acquisition of magic power: In Malaya, the office of magician is hereditary. But occult potency may also be acquired, by contact with the ghost of a murdered man and by performing prescribed rites at his grave.

Actorius: A magic stone, found in capons. When worn round the neck, it confers courage on the owner.

Adamantius: A Jewish physician of Constantinople who, in the reign of Constantine, wrote on the occult art of physiognomy.

Adam Weishaupt: An eighteenth century Illuminatus, or adept in magic.

Aeromancy: Divination by means of atmospheric conditions.

Afreet: In Eastern lore, a demon, the soul of a dead person.

Agamede: A witch mentioned in Homer's Iliad.

Agla: A Kabalistic term—formed of the initial letters of the Hebrew: Aieth Gadol Leolam Adonai—God will be great forever—that was used in invoking demons.

Aglaphotis: An Arabian herb, used by magicians to conjure demons.

Agrafena-Shiganskaia: A Siberian witch, responsible for inducing an extreme nervous condition in women.

Agrippa von Nettesheim (1486-1535): Henry Cornelius Agrippa von Nettesheim, one of the most dominant personalities in the field of the occult, was a soldier, physician, and magician, in contact with the most famous savants of his time. His life was a sequence of honor and misfortune, wealth and poverty. Traveling in France, England, and Italy, he had military and diplomatic experience, held court positions, fell readily into disfavor, and was once imprisoned for debt in Brussels. In Italy he lectured on Hermes Trismegistus; but he came into conflict with the Inquisition.

His major work is The Occult Philosophy, a defense of magic, in which he attempts a synthesis of the natural sciences with occult lore. In spite of his vast knowledge of magic, Agrippa stresses the significance of religion as an aid in magic. But to him religion was an amalgam of Christian elements, Neo-Platonic theory, and Kabalistic mysticism.

Ahriman: In Zoroastrianism, the spirit of evil responsible for the operations of Black Magic.

Akiba: A Jewish rabbi of the first century A.D., believed to have been skilled in magic.

Akkadian-Chaldean Inscriptions: These are the oldest magical documents known. They belonged to the Royal Library of Nineveh, and were engraved in Akkadian, together with Assyrian translations, in the reign of Assurbanipal, in the seventh century B.C. In the form of invocations to the gods of the heavens and the lower regions, the inscriptions are exorcisms against evil of all kinds: sickness, plague, and demons.

Alastor: A monstrous demon.

Albertus Magnus (circa 1206-1280): A theologian who became Bishop of Ratisbon. His reputation as a philosopher was European, yet he had a deep intellectual inquisitiveness about the occult sciences. For the purpose of scientific truth, he experimented with magic and produced remarkable phenomena. His voluminous writings include a survey of alchemy, in which he gives specific directions for the alchemist's conduct. He accepts the reality of the magic virtues of herbs, plants, and stones as healing agents, stimulants of dreams, and antidotes for inebriation. It was said that Albertus Magnus possessed the philosopher's stone for the transmutation of metals, and that he could change atmospheric conditions, even the seasons, at will. Among his productions was an android, an automaton that he endowed with speech.

Alchemy: An art, based partly on mysticism and partly on experimentation, that aimed at the transmutation of metals. It appears to have developed from the second century A.D. onward, reaching its apogee in the Middle Ages. Even as late as the seventeenth century many European scholars, holding university chairs, accepted the truth of alchemical transmutations.

Aldinach: An Egyptian demon that presided over storms, earthquakes, and other cataclysmic forces.

Alectryomancy: Divination by means of a cock that pecked grain placed on letters of the alphabet. There is a vivid description of this practice in The Ides of March, by Thornton Wilder.

Alesteir Crowley (1875-1947): A British Satanist who founded a mystic cult based on magic and occult principles and opposed violently to Christian doctrine. He established a Satanic temple in London, and also in Italy. He was editor of an occult periodical and also produced poetry and expositions on magic themes. Crowley claimed that he was a reincarnation of Edward Kelley, the associate of Dr. John Dee. At his death, a ritual of black magic was performed over his grave by his adherents.

Aleuromancy: Divination from flour. Messages enclosed in balls of dough and prophetic of the future. This is still a practice among the Chinese.

Alexandria: According to Arabian legend, when the city of Alexandria was being built, Alexander the Great used magic talismans to protect it against the nightly attacks of sea monsters.

Algol: An Arabic term for the Devil.

Alice Kyteler: Lady Kyteler was an Irish witch of the fourteenth century who was tried on charges of poisoning her four husbands and practicing sorcery. The record of her trial, like that of many women accused of witchcraft, is preserved in historical archives.

All Hallow's Eve: A festival, also known as Halloween, that takes place on the night of October 31. Of Druidic origin, it is associated with supernatural situations, when witches and demons foregather, and the spirits of the dead wander abroad. The festival involves Saman, the Lord of Death, who, according to Druid traditions, at this time summoned the souls of evil men who had been condemned to dwell in animal bodies. Many customs practiced during All Hallow's Eve, in Ireland and particularly in Northern Scotland, still retain elements of the old Druidic nocturnal rites.

Allison Gross: In Scottish ballad literature, an ugly witch who casts spells on those who do not yield to her.

Alocer: A powerful demon.

Alomancy: Divination by means of salt.

Alphitomancy: A method of divination similar to aleuro-mancy. Wheat or barley cakes were used as a kind of trial by ordeal. The guilty person could not swallow such cakes and was consequently condemned.

Alphonse Louis Constant (1809-1875): A Frenchman who under the name of Eliphas Lévi wrote a series of books on magic.

Altrunes: Among the ancient Teutonic tribes, female demons believed to have been of Hun origin.

Amniomancy: Divination by observation of the caul on a child's head at birth.

Amulet: This word stems from an Arabic root meaning 'to carry.' The amulet is something carried or worn upon the person. Amulets are of two kinds: those inscribed with magic formulae, and those not so inscribed.

The amulet is an object worn as a protection against black magic, the evil eye, imprisonment, loss of property, and similar calamities. The inscribed formula may be in the nature of a geometric design, written on clay, metal, parchment, or deerskin. Or the object itself may be a gem, or the tail of a fox, a lizard, a chameleon, a mandrake, or colored threads; a ring, a nail, a key, or a knot. One of the most frequent types of formula is the magic square:

4	9	2
3	5	7
8	1	6

The arrangement is such that the sum of the numbers in each row, taken perpendicularly, horizontally, and diagonally, is identical.

An amulet or talisman against nightmares, incubi, and succubi was a device of a scorpion whose body was covered with a mystic inscription. Another amulet used in banishing nightmares consisted of secret symbols written on pieces of paper, crushed into a ball, and swallowed. In Hebraic lore, a Kamea was an amulet consisting of a written parchment, called Pitka, or a small bundle of plants. An effective charm against sorcery was three grains of madder. The snout of a wolf, fixed on a door, served an apotropaic purpose.

Certain talismans, again, were efficacious on specific days of the week, and the efficacy was determined by astrological computation.

Amulets have special effectiveness, too, in association with burial-grounds and crossroads. Thus a bone or a plant or herb found in such a spot had a particular potency.

Amy: A powerful demon, one of the rulers of the infernal regions.

Anachitis: A stone used in conjuring water spirits.

Anancithidus: A stone used in conjuring demons.

Ananisapta: A Kabalistic term inscribed on parchment as a talisman against disease.

Ancient Britain: The three most famous sorcerers of Ancient Britain were Menw, Eiddilic the Dwarf and Math.

Androalpha: An arch-demon of the Infernal Empire.

Anduscias: A powerful demon.

Angakok: An Eskimo witch-doctor.

Angat: In Madagascar, the name for the Devil, in the form of a serpent.

Angurvadel: In Icelandic legend, a sword possessed of magic properties.

Animals: In ancient times, certain creatures were always associated with magic rites. These included the owl, hyena, frog, mole, lizard, chameleon, weasel.

Animate, inanimate: The practice of turning inanimate objects into living creatures and back into inanimate objects was common among magicians in the East from very ancient times onward.

Anointing oil: Witches anointed themselves with oil consisting of vervain or mint crushed and steeped in olive oil, left overnight, then squeezed through a cloth. The squeezing was repeated several times until ready for use.

Ansuperomin: A sorcerer who, in the reign of Henry IV of France, was notorious in Sabbat assemblies.

Anthropomancy: Divination by means of consultation of the intestines of sacrificed children. This method is said to have been used by the Emperor Julian the Apostate, who practiced necromancy.

Anthropophagism: The eating of human flesh. In the Middle Ages witches were credited with eating human flesh. The Lex Salica, sanctioned by Clovis I in the sixth century, condemns any witch convicted of such an act to a fine of two hundred gold pennies.

Antipalus Maleficiorum: A treatise on magic by the mediaeval demonographer Trithemius.

Antipathes: A black coral anciently used for apotropaic purposes in magic.

Apantomancy: Divination by observation of objects that appear haphazardly.

Apep: In Egyptian demonology, a monstrous demon, usually represented as a crocodile, that could be destroyed by making a wax figure of him and burning it. Apep led the other demons in an assault against the Sun.

Apollonius of Tyana: A Greek philosopher of the first century A.D. who traveled widely, as far as India, in search of esoteric knowledge. In the course of his wanderings he lectured to his disciples, relating his experiences with goblins, spirits, vampires, and other occult phenomena. He thus acquired a formidable reputation as a thaumaturgist. In Asia Minor, in fact, temples were dedicated to him as to a deity. Brought to Rome, Apollonius was tried on a charge of practicing divination from the entrails of a boy sacrificed for the purpose. The latter years of his life are obscure.

In the Middle Ages the name of Apollonius was associated with endless legends and stories on magic themes, and Apollonius himself was considered the Archmagician.

Apuleius: A Roman writer of the second century A.D., who wrote a picaresque novel packed with fantastic episodes: magic transformations, mysterious dream sequences, occult rites, enchantments, and other varieties of witchcraft. A certain witch, declares one of the characters, can bring down heaven, hang up the earth, exorcise the dead. By incantations, rapid rivers can be made to run backward, oceans can be congealed, winds robbed of breath, the sun stopped in its course, the moon made to drop its foam, stars plucked from their spheres, day annihilated, night indefinitely prolonged.

Apuleius himself, accused of securing a wife through magic practice, wrote and delivered a speech in his defense, in which he discussed the field of magic. This speech, still extant, is a vast mine of information on occult techniques.

Arbatel: A manual of magic, published in the sixteenth century.

Ardat-Lile: A Semitic female demon that copulated with human males.

Ariolist: A diviner by means of an altar.

Armomancy: Divination by observation of the shoulders of a sacrificial animal.

Arnold of Villanova: A thirteenth century physician who traveled in Europe and Africa. He was interested in the occult, the interpretation of dreams, and alchemy. He is said to have made transmutations before eye-witnesses. Even in his medical practice he relied largely on Kabalistic symbols, occult invocations, and herbal concoctions of magic significance. He was also reputed to have facile communication with the Satanic powers.

Arnuphis: An Egyptian sorcerer of the second century A.D.

Arphaxat: A Persian sorcerer.

Arrows: A means of prognostication, known in Biblical times. "The king of Babylon stood at the parting of the way, at the head of the two ways, to use divination; he made his arrows bright, he consulted with images, he looked in the liver." Ezekiel 21:21.

On the arrows were written the names of enemies. The king shook up the arrows in the quiver and the arrow he drew out was directed at the enemy whose name had been inscribed on it.

Artephius: A twelfth century Hermetic, reputed to have lived more than a thousand years, by demoniac aid. Sometimes he is confused with Apollonius of Tyana. Artephius wrote The Art of Prolonging Life, allegedly at the age of 1025.

Asaphin: A Chaldean sorcerer and diviner.

Ascletarion: A sorcerer who foretold that the Emperor would be devoured by dogs: which actually occurred, after Domitian's death.

Ashes: Magic ashes, for purification purposes, are described in Numbers 19.1. The ashes are those of a red, unblemished heifer that has been sacrificed.

Asiza: In African Dahomey, spirits who dwell in the forests and give magic powers to man.

Asmodeus: In Hebraic legend, king of the demons. His

queen was Lilith. Pictorially, Asmodeus is represented with three heads, goose feet, a snake's tail. Among his activities are making men invisible and revealing hidden treasures.
Aspidomancy: Divination by sitting on a shield, within a magic circle. While uttering conjurations, the practitioner · falls into a trance and pronounces mantic revelations.
Ass: Among the Romans the ass was an evil omen, but it was honored among the Arabs.
Astragalomancy: Divination by means of knucklebones.
Athame: A black-hilted consecrated knife, with magic symbols inscribed on the handle, used by witches for drawing a magic circle to invoke demons.
Atharvaveda: Hindu sacred literature that contains magical recitations used for apotropaic purposes.
Augustin Calmet (1672-1756): A French Benedictine monk who in 1751 published a book on witchcraft, demonology, and vampires.
Austatikco-Pauligaur: In Persian demonology, monstrous demons.
Avenar: A fifth century A.D. Jewish astrologer, who computed the coming of a Hebraic Messiah.
Axinomancy: Divination by means of an axe.
Aza: Aza and Azael were chiefs of the fallen angels who taught magic to men.
Azazel: A powerful demon, dweller in the desert, and associated with ancient Hebraic rites. The name also appears in Greek magical papyri and in the mediaeval grimoires.

B

Baalzaphon: A demon, one of the rulers of the infernal regions.

Bacis: An ancient Greek seer, of Boeotia, mentioned by Cicero. Anyone with mantic pretensions often assumed the name of Bacis.

Backward magic: Recitations of certain formulae or passages, backward, in order to counteract or produce magic effects. Incantations were chanted backward, mystical names reversed, words written backward. In Western Europe, the Pater Noster was said backward by the Satanists, devotees of the Arch Demon. The recital of a particular formula backward could give a person the power to assume any shape he desired.

Bacoti: Among the Tonkinese, a sorceress and necromancer.

Balan: A powerful demon in the infernal hierarchy.

Barau: In Polynesian demonology, a sorcerer.

Barbatos: A demon, associated with forests, who knows the past and the future and has beneficent tendencies.

Bar-Ligura: A Hebraic demon that haunts house tops.

Barsom: A bunch of tamarind, pomegranate, or date twigs carried by the ancient priests of Persia as a protective agent against witches and demons.

Bascanie: A kind of fascinatio used by Greek magicians. The effect was to make a person see opposites: a black object appearing as white, a pretty face ugly.

Basilides: Founder of a Gnostic sect. He belonged to Alexandria, in the second century A.D.

Bath of Immortality: A regime for ensuring immortality, according to the wizard Menander, the successor to Simon Magus.

Batsaum-Pasha: A Turkish demon, invoked to secure fine weather, or rain.

Bayemon: A powerful demon, monarch in the Infernal Regions.

Beans: Among the Egyptians, beans were endowed with magical properties. Among the ancients, black beans were presented as an offering to the infernal gods. Pythagoras used beans in his magic experiments.

Bechard: A demon who controls winds and storms.

Beelzebub: Lord of Flies, the Prince of Demons, represented as a monstrous fly. Among the ancient Canaanites a temple was dedicated to his worship.

Bees: According to demonographers, eating the queen bee was a means of enduring torture without confessing to the practice of witchcraft.

Belephantes: A Chaldean astrologer. According to the historian Diodorus Siculus he rightly predicted that Alexander the Great's entry into Babylon would be fatal to the Emperor.

Belief in witchcraft: Such belief was held, not as a vulgar superstition, but as a scrupulously observed science, by kings and queens, among them Queen Elizabeth of England and James VI of Scotland, statesmen and university authorities, medical men, theologians, and writers.

In regard to the actual practice of wizardry, apart from professional magicians, kings and queens, princelings and prelates and popes dabbled or were suspected of dabbling in the Black Arts: among them Catherine de Medici, Henry III, Pope Leo the Great, Pope Sixtus V, and the Duc de Richelieu.

Belocolus: A stone reputed to confer invisibility on the field of battle.

Belomancy: Divination by means of arrows.

Belphegor: A demon with gaping mouth, bearded, and phallic-like tongue, worshipped obscenely. In Hindu demonology, he is Rutrem, a monstrous Priapus.

Benemmerinnen: Semitic demons who harass women in childbirth with the intention of stealing the child.

Benjees: Devil worshippers of the East Indies.

Berosus of Cos: An astrologer of the first century A.D., to whom a large number of grimoires were popularly ascribed.

Bezoar: A precious stone, found in the entrails of certain animals, possessing magical properties.

Bibliomancy: Divination by consultation of chapters or lines in a book, selected at random.

Bibliothèque de l'Arsenal de Paris: This library contains manuscripts of mediaeval grimoires and other treatises on Black Magic.

Bifrons: A demon skilled in geometry, herbal lore, and astrology.

Billis: African sorcerers, capable of preventing the growth of rice.

Birds: In Malayan magic, certain birds, particularly nocturnal birds such as the night owl and the shroud-tearer, prognosticate death by their harsh notes.

Bitabas: In African demonology, a sorcerer.

Black Books: Grimoires, or manuals on magic in its multiple manifestations. Among the most remarkable Black Books are:

The Grimoire of Pope Honorius, the earliest printed copy of which is dated 1629, at Rome.

Little Albert.

Red Dragon.

Hell's Coercion, attributed to Dr. Faustus.

The Great Grimoire.

Sanctum Regum.

The Black Pullet.

The Great and Powerful Sea Ghost, by Dr. Johann Faustus.

Black Magic, White Magic: Distinctions have been drawn by some demonographers, and by practitioners themselves, on the basis that White Magic has an ethical motive, while Black Magic aims at evil effects. But this distinction is merely verbal, and is forthrightly condemned by Montague

Summers the demonographer. Wallis Budge, the Egyptologist, on the other hand, declares that Egyptian magic has two purposes: to benefit the living and the dead: or to act maleficently against victims and enemies.

Black Mass: The mass held in honor of the Devil at the Witches' Sabbat and on other occasions. In the supersophisticated French society of seventeenth century Paris, it was conducted to the accompaniment of obscene rites, fantastically garbed officiants, while the Mass itself was said over the nude body of a woman.

Pictorially, the mediaeval Black Mass was awesome and impressive, and has consequently been the subject of many paintings, etchings, and sculptures. Against a dark, wooded horizon, in an open area, stood an altar of stone, with a large, black-stained wooden image of Satan, goat-formed, adorning it. Between the horns of the figure a torch flared. Ceremonials lasted from late at night until the early hours. Crops and animals were sacrificed. A priestess, usually a young girl, embraced the phallus of the image. A banquet followed, with wine, beer, and cider flowing abundantly. Then came a Sabbat dance, with the participants dancing back to back, contorting themselves into Satanic ecstasy by febrile gyrations and obscene caperings, to an obbligato of tambourines, fifes, violins, drums, horns, or theorbos.

Well-known rendezvous of the Black Mass were the Brocken, in the Hartz Mountains of Germany, and in the church of Blokula, in Sweden. The artist Goya has excellently realized the wild, occult nature of these dark rites.

Blacksmith: In Abyssinian legend, blacksmiths were considered sorcerers.

Blasting Rod: A rod used by magicians for smiting and subduing spirits. In the Lemegeton a hazel stick is to be used similarly for driving a demon into the magic triangle.

Bloodstone: A magic stone that gave its owner the power of having his wishes fulfilled.

Bocal: A priest-sorcerer in the reign of Henry IV. Accused of attending a Black Mass, he was condemned to death.

All the members of his family were reputed to be Satanists.

Bogomils: The Bogomils, Children of Satanael, were mediaeval Satanists associated with Central European regions.

Bokor: A Haitian magician who controls the spirits of the dead.

Book of Ballymote: A fourteenth century Irish book that contains an outline of a course in magic, with instruction in enchantments.

Book of Death: A black book in which, during the Witches' Sabbat, the Devil inscribed the names of the assembled witches.

Book of the Sacred Magic of Abramelin the Mage as delivered by Abraham the Jew unto his son Lamech: A sixteenth century text, originally written in Hebrew, that is virtually a picaresque tale of magicians, magic, and occult practices.

Borgia: Cesare Borgia was reputed to have had a familiar.

Botanomancy: Divination by burning branches of brier and vervain, on which were inscribed questions to be answered.

Brimstone: According to Pliny the Elder, brimstone was used in Roman houses to divert evil spirits.

Brizomancy: Divination by the inspiration of Brizo, a goddess of sleep.

Broxa: A mediaeval demon, or witch. As a witch, it is maleficent and reads the future. Similar to the estrie, the broxa is capable of changing shape at will. It flies about at night on evil missions, and drinks human blood like a vampire.

Brujo (feminine: Bruja): In Cuban demonology, a sorcerer.

Bruxa: A Portuguese term for a witch.

Bucon: A demon mentioned in the Key of Solomon.

Buer: A beneficent demon who brought domestic happiness and health.

Bulwer-Lytton (1831-1891): An English novelist who was interested in the occult and was acquainted with Eliphas Lévi. In one of his futuristic novels, The Coming Race,

Lytton refers to an occult essence, vril, which has astral significance. Lytton was at one time the head of a centre of magic in London.

Bune: A demon that haunts tombs.

Byleth: A demon: one of the kings of the Infernal Regions.

C

Caaerinolaas: The Grand President of Hell.

Cabiri: Ancient deities, associated with Samothrace and other districts of Greece; noted for their magic powers.

Caduceus: Mercury's wand, with two entwined serpents, symbolizing the powers of magic.

Caesar of Heisterbach: A German Cistercian monk of the thirteenth century who wrote a Dialogue on Miracles in twelve books. This is a collection of dramatically presented legends about occult practices, and particularly about the manifestations of the Devil, in both human and animal form, among men.

Cagliostro (1745-1795): Count Alessandro Cagliostro, an Italian alchemist, Hermetic, and magician, was really, beneath his fictitious title, Giuseppe Balsamo. Fleeing from Sicily after committing a number of crimes, he began to travel over Europe, studying alchemy and sorcery. So skilled did he become that he was welcomed among the most notable families of the continent. With his wife Lorenza Feliciani he continued his wanderings, amassing enormous wealth through the sale of magic elixirs, love potions, and alchemical compounds. Implicated in many scandals, Cagliostro was forced to move often and abruptly over Europe. He experienced so many adventures that his name acquired a legendary fame. His last years he spent in imprisonment, in the fortress of San Leo.

Among his recorded feats are the production of a diamond by alchemical means and the conjuration of a dead woman. At one banquet Cagliostro summoned the putative spirits of many famous men, including Diderot and Voltaire. He also founded a secret society called The Egyptian Lodge, noted for its magic séances.

Calundronius: A magic stone that resists demons and nullifies enchantments.

Calypso: A nymph who appears in Homer's epic poem the Odyssey. She has the power of conferring immortality. (See: **Homer**).

Cambions: The offspring of succubi and incubi.

Canidia: A witch who appears in one of the poems by the Roman poet Horace. She is described as torturing a child to death in order to use his marrow and spleen in a love-potion for herself.

Capnomancy: Divination by means of wreaths of smoke.

Captromancy: Divination by means of the fumes rising from poppy thrown on live coals.

Catabolics: These were demons who kidnapped and killed men.

Catalin: A wizard who appears frequently in Irish magic legend.

Catancy: A plant used by Thessalian witches in love-philtres.

Catherine La Voisin: A witch, fortune-teller, and dispenser of philtres, who was intimately associated with the occult operations of Madame de Montespan.

Catoptromancy: Divination by means of a lens or a magic mirror. This technique was known to the ancients, and is mentioned by Apuleius, Pausanias the Greek traveler, and St. Augustine.

Catoptromancy was practiced by the Dyaks of Borneo and the Incas.

Cats: The cat, "the first pet of civilization," has always been associated with magical powers. Of all animals, the cat alone looks one in the eye. The glance of the cat can terrify, and such a fear is known as ailurophobia. Hitler had a fear of cats. When Napoleon saw a cat stalking through his palace, he called for help. Joseph Bonaparte, King of Naples, while on a visit to Saratoga Springs in 1825, collapsed in a guest's house. He had sensed a cat's presence, although no animal was visible. A search produced a kitten hiding in a sideboard. Henry III used to faint at the sight of a cat. Buffon, the French naturalist, dreaded the animal: as did Oliver Goldsmith, and James Boswell. Albert Einstein, on the other hand, was fond of cats. So was that strange character Lafcadio Hearn. Pierre Loti, the French novelist, had calling cards printed for his own pets.

The cat was sacred in ancient India. In Sanskrit literature, frequent reference is made to the animal and to its influence on man. In ancient Britain the cat, probably introduced by the Romans, had great prestige, with attendant sacred rites in its honor. Hywel Dda, a prince of South Wales, enacted a law, in the tenth century, for the protection of cats.

But it was the Egyptians who raised the cat to supreme divinity. The Egyptian word for tomcat is kut, while a tabby is kutta. The cat, as a deity, was the "Sayer of Great Words." Hence killing a cat was punishable by death. In Lower Egypt an entire city, Bubastis, was dedicated to cat worship. The feeding of these sacred animals was itself a high privilege. The cats fed on catfish. Every year, some 700,000 pilgrims journeyed to Bubastis to the cat festival in May. There was music, and wine ran copiously. The temples were packed with penitents making vows to the cat deities. Cat amulets were on sale in public booths: figurines of cats in amethyst, calcite, and red cornelian.

Among cat goddesses, the most prominent was Ubasti, represented in bronze as a cat-headed woman. Prayers and sacrifices were part of the ritual of cat worship. After death, cats were embalmed and shipped to Bubastis for burial.

When the Egyptian cat cult died out, cat influence, still potent, spread to Europe, where Cat Clans sprang up in Celtic and Teutonic regions. In the first century B.C. the cat motif was dominant. Roman legionary soldiers bore a cat sign on their shields. The crest of the Germanic tribe of Catti was a brindled cat. The Cattani of Scotland likewise had a cat on their crest.

The last remaining Cat Clan is still in force, in the Scottish Highlands, where the Clan Chattan, a federation of clans originally formed to settle disputes among member clans, holds sway. Several of these clans bear on their crest the motto: Touch not the cat bot (that is, without a glove). Popularly, the members of the Clan Chattan are known as the People of the Cat.

In Scandinavian countries Freya is the cat-goddess. She is depicted as drawn in a chariot by two cats. Girls contrived to wed on Freya's Day—Friday. If the day was sunny, it was said that the bride had fed the cat well.

In Europe in the Middle Ages, cats, preferably black, were associated with nocturnal magic. Along with witches, cats were tortured as purveyors of evil. Cats were even believed capable of speaking the language of their mistresses. There was an eighteenth century English witch, Moll White, whose cat was reputed to have talked in English. The cat was also a symbol of efficiency, and was consequently selected by European business men as a trademark.

Cat influence is so rooted in folkways that all kinds of expressions are derived from cat associations. In mediaeval times a movable penthouse used in siege works was called a cat—from the slow, catlike approach of the engine of war. A cat-o-nine-tails tells its own story. Cat's eyes are considered, in humans, magnetic and exotic. An old Massachusetts law warns owners against keeping a cat out of doors at night under penalty of a stiff fine.

Cauldron: In Celtic lore, a kettle or cauldron used in magic rites: to restore the dead or to bring fertility to crops. At the Sabbat assemblies it was also used for brewing poisons and philtres.

Cauldron of Regeneration: A witch ceremony, held on or near December 12: also called Drawing Down the Moon. Into a cauldron set in the middle of a magic circle are thrown leaves, over which spirit is poured and ignited. The members present, led by the witch-priestess, chant an invocation to the Moon, dancing in ecstasy and exclaiming:

Io! Evohoe!
Blessed be Io Evohoe!

This is an invocation to Bacchus, the wine god, the god of fertility. The rite, practised in twentieth-century England, is described in Witchcraft Today.

Causimomancy: Divination by means of fire. It was a good omen when objects, thrown into a fire, did not burn.

Cellini (1500-1571): Benvenuto Cellini, an Italian artist, goldsmith, and sculptor, describes in his autobiography a conjuration of spirits performed in Rome, at which he was present, together with a number of acknowledged sorcerers.

Cephalomancy: Divination by means of a donkey's head.

Cepionidus: A magic stone that reflects the image of the beholder.

Ceramancy: Divination by interpretation of melted wax dropped on the floor.

Ceraunoscopy: An ancient method of divination by observation of the phenomena of the air, thunder, and lightning.

Cerne: An obsolete name for the magic circle made by the magician's wand to conjure demons.

Chair of Magic: In the Middle Ages, Toledo, in Spain, was known for its interest in witchcraft. It is even said to have had at its university a professorship of Black Magic, the course in the occult arts lasting for seven years.

Chaldea: A country that was particularly rich and dominantly active in magic cults and rituals. As early as the Book of Daniel the term Chaldeans, Kasdim, was equated with magicians. The Romans, too, called astrologers and adepts in the black arts by the generic name of Chaldeans. In the first century A.D. the Greek Strabo refers to the astrological skill of the Chaldeans.

Cham-Zoroaster: Traditionally considered to have been the first magician, after the period of the Flood.

Change of name: In the Middle Ages a sick person often changed his name, with the intention of diverting and confusing the spirit responsible for the malady.

Characteristics of magic: Certain features are characteristic in all magic rites. These include: the color black, nudity, dishevelled hair, bare feet.

Charles Hacks: A nineteenth century physician, of German extraction, who, under the pseudonym of Dr. Bataille, is presumed to have written Le Diable au xixe siècle, in which the author recounts strange personal occult experiences and deals with the wide prevalence of Satanism.

Charm: A magic formula or object that is effective in producing potent results: as Aladdin's lamp, or the formula "Open Sesame." According to Apuleius, fish were often used as love-charms.

Chiromancy: An occult art that evaluates the lines of a person's hand with a view to interpreting his character and destiny.

Christianity and Witchcraft: After the introduction of Christianity into Britain, pagan rites, according to St. Augustine, still survived. Even as late as the seventh century Archbishop Theodore forbade the offering of sacrifices to Devils, the eating in heathen temples, the celebrating of feasts in abominable places, and the dressing of people in animal skins. All these injunctions were directed against the prevalent practices of witches.

Chyndonax: An ancient Druid priest-magician.

Cicero: Marcus Tullius Cicero, the Roman orator and philosopher, who flourished in the first century B.C., wrote a treatise on Divination, in which he discusses magical songs, incantations, and similar topics.

Ciupipiltin: Malevolent spirits of women who died at childbirth.

Cledonomancy: Divination by observation of utterances of mantic significance.

Cleidomancy: Divination by means of a key hanging by a thread from a young girl's third finger nail.

Cleromancy: Divination by means of drawing lots.

Cobolis: Among the ancient Sarmatians, demons.

Cockcrow: The Sabbat assembly always ended at cockcrow.

College of Druids: Such a training centre was said to exist as late as the sixth century A.D., on the "Isle of the Druids," in the Hebridean Isles off Scotland.

Colors: Pliny the Elder declares that auguries and omens were drawn from the color of the sun's rays, from the moon, the planets, and the air.

Compusa: A female succuba demon.

Conception-billets: These were billets of consecrated paper which, when swallowed, dispelled disease. When placed in a child's cradle, the billet acted as a guard against witchcraft. The billet was also attached to domestic articles, placed in barns and under thresholds, for the same purpose.

During the Middle Ages, these conception-billets were sold for small sums by the Carmelite monks.

Conjuration: A typical formula, after the officiant has placed himself in the magic circle, runs thus:

> I—the name of the sorcerer is here given—conjure you, spirit—mentioned by name, in the name of the great living God, I conjure you to appear before me. If not, Saint Michael the archangel, invisible, will strike you into the bottommost depths of hell. Come then—spirit again named—to do my bidding.

Constitution of Honorius: A book on magic attributed to Pope Honorius III, whose floruit is the thirteenth century, and first published early in the seventeenth century. It describes in detail the ritual in conjuration: involving mutilation of a black cock, sacrifice of a lamb, the inscription of mystic symbols.

Copper: According to Theocritus, this metal possesses the power of banishing spirits. Whenever a Spartan ruler died, the Spartans beat on a copper pot.

Corneto: There is an ancient Etruscan necropolis at Corneto, which is not far from Civita Vecchia, Italy, where excavations have revealed paintings depicting the conjuration of demons.

Coscinomancy: Divination by means of sieves.

Cotton Mather (1663-1728): A Boston minister, notorious for his violent participation in the Salem, New England, witch-hunts of the seventeenth century.

Coven: A society or club of witches, usually consisting of thirteen members, the thirteenth being the leader. Symbolically, this thirteenth member was Satan himself. Sodalities consisting of only ten, seven, or three members are also on record. Each coven was independent, but was associated with other covens under a Grand Master, who represented Satan Incarnate himself. There are still a few covens in existence in present-day England and on the European continent.

Numerology plays a significant role in the economy of the coven, the numbers 3, 5, 8, 13, 40 being particularly significant. 40 means three covens and one leader. 13 means two pairs of sympathetic members, usually husband and wife, and one leader or priestess. The members have passwords as a means of recognition, although usually they know each other. In Italian covens the password is 6 and 7, that is 13.

Coven (origin): The term coven derives from covent or convent, a religious assembly. In the course of time the religious implication of the abbreviated form, coven, disappeared.

Craca: A witch mentioned by the historian Saxo Grammaticus, who changed food into stones.

Critomancy: Divination by observing the paste of cakes and the barley flour sprinkled over the victims in a sacrifice.

Cromniomancy: Divination by means of onions placed on the altar on Christmas Day.

Crow: At the Sabbat, in the invocation to the Devil, the celebrant cries: Black crow! Black crow!

Cubomancy: Divination by thimbles. This was an ancient Greek technique. It was also practiced, among the Romans, by the Emperors Augustus and Tiberius.

Cups: Cups possessing magic properties appear in Celtic legend. The Quadrangular Cup of the Fenians gave a person any drink he desired. Other magic cups cured dumbness, or brought good luck.

D

Dactyliomancy: Divination by means of a finger-ring.

Dactyls: Legendary Phrygian wizards.

Danis: A famous eighteenth century sorcerer.

Daphnomancy: Divination by observing the way in which a laurel branch burns and crackles in a fire.

Darts: Lapland magicians used magic darts that, when hurled, carried with them agonies and injuries to the victim.

Dead Bodies: In ancient Thessaly the dead were scrupulously guarded at night, as the witches were in the habit of tearing off, with their teeth, pieces of flesh from the corpse, for use in magic spells.

Demons: Malevolent spirits, "messengers of Satan," bent on destruction. They are usually equipped with wings, know the future, can move over the entire earth, eat, drink, propagate, and die. They can see, but remain invisible. These agencies, that include the spirits of the dead, find their most propitious time for action in the darkness of night. They constantly assail human beings in a variety of sinister ways, even entering the human body. As a protection against such operations, amulets, spells, and incantations, together with certain occult ceremonials, are used by the victim. Among the efficacious media that demons abhor are fire, light, water, and spittle; as well as salt, bread, herbs; also the digital sexual gesture of the "fig."

According to John Wierus, the number of demons reaches about seven and a quarter million, who are controlled by some seventy-nine higher powers.

Demons as agents: Demons were sent to avenge or punish human evils, according to Ecclesiasticus 39.33:

> There are spirits that are created for vengeance, and in their fury they lay on grievous torments.

As agents of wizards, demons have special functions. Strabo, the Greek geographer, declares that demons traverse the world, driven by the incantations of witches, for the purpose of collecting various seeds that make certain species grow that witches use in philtres and similar concoctions.
Deserts: Extensive abandoned space is always associated with demons. Maimonides, a mediaeval philosopher, declares "In those days the belief had spread that spirits dwelt in the desert, spoke, and appeared there."
Devil's Baton: Such a staff, said to have been used by the Devil himself, is preserved in Tolentino, Italy.
Devil's Bell: In the Pyrenees, the ringing of bells was associated with demoniac operations.
Devil's Bread: The Dutch call mushrooms by this name.
Devil's characteristics: In spite of the sinister and malevolent reputation of the Arch Fiend, the Devil, in mediaeval legend, is credited with occasional good deeds and services toward man. In anthropomorphic form, he becomes the builder of bridges that human engineering skill cannot achieve. Or he works in silver mines where human miners cannot penetrate. Or, as a navigator, he steers ships through tremendous hazards.
Devil's Dance: In Tibet, in other regions of the Orient, and in Africa, the devil dance, in which there is impersonation of demons by means of devil masks, is a means of exorcism.
Devil's Girdle: In the Middle Ages, witches were accused of wearing such an article.
Devil's Signature: In the Bibliothèque Nationale in Paris there is a letter in French signed by Asmodeus and dated Nineteenth of May, 1629.

In one of the Black Books of Magic, the Grand Grimoire, there is a bond made between the magician and the demon, signed by Lucifuge Rofocale.
Devil Worshippers: Yesidi means "God-worshipper," but the name of devil worshippers is applied to the small Yesidi

community of the Sinjar Hills, in Iraq, that claims descent from Adam alone.

Diadochus: A gem that had properties conducive to divination.

Diancecht: In Irish legend, god of leechcraft, master of wizardry, who possessed a magic copper boat called The Wave-Sweeper.

Diodorus of Catania: A sorcerer and magician notorious for his power of the evil eye. He was burned alive in an oven.

Disease: Among the Romans, amulets were used to prevent or dispel diseases of the eye, headaches, toothache, tumors, epilepsy, fevers, and poisonous bites.

Div: The Iranian term for demons.

Divination: The practice of gaining knowledge of the unknown or the future by consulting spirits, examining entrails of animals, interpreting dreams and atmospheric conditions, and similar occult means. Insects and animals can also be used in divination, as the bearers of occult messages.

Among the Arabs, one method of divination involves drawing lines in the sand.

Divining cup: A cup used in the interpretation of the future. The cup mentioned in Genesis 44:5, in connection with the story of Joseph, was probably such a cup.

Djinn (Jinn): In Moslem demonology, spirits that possess supernatural powers. They are corporeal beings, usually animal shaped, in the form of ostriches, or snakes. They can assume human form as well. They ride on porcupines, foxes, and gazelles.

In Malayan magic, there are 190 Black Djinn, who operate maleficently among the hills and forests.

Dr. Johannes Faustus: A mediaeval German magician, considered the "greatest nigromancer of his age," who wrote a large number of books on magic and himself practiced the occult arts. There is an etching of Dr. Faustus by

Rembrandt showing the wizard at work on some magical operation.

Dogs: Demons often assumed the form of a dog.

Dragon's Blood: Bathing in dragon's blood could restore life or produce invulnerability.

Dreams: Dreams were believed to be of supernatural origin, appearing in the form of visitations by demons, spirits of the dead, and at times beneficent agencies. As prognostications of the future, dreams required a skilled interpreter, as in the case of Joseph at Pharaoh's court.

Throughout Biblical literature, in fact, dreams were tantamount to prognostications, as in the following instances:

Genesis 20.3; Genesis 31.23; Genesis 37.5.

Job 33.15.

Numbers 12.6.

I Kings 3.5.

To the ancient Greeks, dreams had occult significances as being nocturnal messages of the gods. In the second century A.D. Artemidorus of Daldis traveled widely for the sole purpose of collecting dream lore. He later published a book on the interpretation of dreams. Dreams were also interpreted, in the Greek temples, as therapeutic indications, and their interpretations were recorded and used for medical purposes.

The Greek historian Xenophon discusses dreams as a medium of divination.

Dr. John Dee (1527-1608): An English mathematician who also studied, both in England and in Europe, astrology, alchemy, and other occult subjects. He had a stormy career, was imprisoned on charges of casting horoscopes and using enchantments against Queen Mary of England, and acquired a reputation as a magician. He was later sent on government service to Europe and there collaborated with a certain Edward Kelley, a self-styled magician. As the author of Liber Mysteriorum, The Book of Mysteries, Dee surveyed the occult world and confirmed his writings by practicing crystalomancy in order to communicate with the dead.

A magic mirror, or speculum, once the property of Dr. Dee, is now in the British Museum.

Dr. John Harries: A nineteenth century Welsh physician and diviner, who possessed a notorious Book of Magic.

Druids: Ancient Gallic priest-magicians who wove spells and practiced divination and other magic techniques. Druid rites are embodied in All Hallow's Eve as observed in the North of Scotland. In the Scottish Hebridean Islands are to be found the reputed sites of Druid altars dedicated to human sacrifices.

Pliny the Elder, a Roman encyclopedist, declares in his Natural History, Book 16, that the expression Druids is synonymous with magi—a word whose connotation varied between "magicians," "scholars," "philosophers"; but which most probably means in this context "magicians," since Pliny says elsewhere, in Book 30, that magic was so prevalent in Gaul that in the reign of Tiberius, in the first century A.D., a decree was issued against the Druids together with "the whole pack of such physicians, prophets, and wizards."

The Druids appear in Celtic literature as well as in Julius Caesar's Commentaries on the Gallic War. In Irish legend, too, Druids are known as sorcerers, knowledgeable in spells, wizardry, incantations, augury by the flight and song of birds, by dreams, and by examination of the entrails in human sacrifices.

The Druids could control atmospheric conditions and bring down snow, storm, and darkness: cast mist over landscapes, produce visual illusions, induce forgetfulness by secret potions, walk unharmed, barefooted, over beds of burning coal, understand animal language. Many of their more sinister powers they often directed against enemy forces.

The Druidic wand, fashioned from a yew, hawthorn, oak, or rowan, was used in magic transformation. The Druids could assume new shapes—animate and inanimate—at will, and also enchant men into new forms.

Druid's Wheel: Also called the Elucidator. A contraption used in divination.

Druj: In Zoroastrianism, a corpse-fiend.

Drum: In Lapland, magicians invoked their familiars by means of occult rhythmic beating on a drum.

In Malaya, certain sacred royal drums can be struck only by a designated tribe; otherwise the drummer is struck dead.

Drusii: Among the ancient Gauls, demons that copulated with women.

Duc de Richelieu: Apart from his political prominence, the Duc de Richelieu engaged in black magic practices.

Duppy: In the demonology of the West Indies, a ghost.

E

Earl of Bothwell: In the sixteenth century, a Scottish noble who was the Grand Master of a large sodality of witches.

Effectiveness of magic: Although the essential nature of witchcraft is its hypothetical concrete effectiveness, there is on no occasion objective proof of such complete, exclusive efficacy of the magic act.

Eggs: In ancient times, at a meal, eggs were smashed or pierced, so that sorcerers could make use of them in their rites.

Ekimmu: In Assyrian demonology, a vampire-demon.

Elaeomancy: Divination by observation of a liquid surface.

Elias Ashmole: An English alchemist of the seventeenth century.

Eliphas Lévi (circa 1810-1870): A French occultist whose real name was Alphonse Louis Constant. Son of a shoemaker, he was educated for the priesthood, but was expelled for his views. He married a beautiful young girl, but she left him. Devoting himself to occultism, he gave esoteric instruction to disciples. He himself professed to have conjured the spirit of Apollonius of Tyana. Among other writings, he produced a History of Witchcraft, written with literary imagination and a sense of wonderment, and emphasizing metaphysical and mystical interpretations of the principles affecting the arcana of Nature.

Elymas: Also called Bar-Jesus. A sorcerer who appears in the Bible:

"And there (in Paphos) they came across a Jewish magician and false prophet named Bar-Jesus." Acts 13.6.

Emerald Tablet: A tablet, said to have been found by Alexander the Great in the tomb of Hermes, and reputedly written by Hermes, in which the essence of magic is revealed.

Empusae: Ancient obscene and malevolent female demons, offspring of Hecate. They could assume animal shape, but often appeared as beautiful maidens, who acted as succubae. They are mentioned by the Greek comedy writer Aristophanes.

Empyromancy: Divination by observation of objects placed on a sacrificial fire.

Ephesian Letters: Ancient Greek expressions used to ward off enchantments: e.g. aski, kataski, tetrax.

Ephod: A garment used by the priests of Israel as a means of oracular knowledge. The Ephod Oracle was consulted by King Saul and King David.

Erichtho: A witch who practiced monstrous black arts, including necromancy. She appears in the Roman poet Lucan's epic poem, the Pharsalia.

Eromancy: A Persian method of divination by exposing objects to the air.

Erotylos: A stone that, according to Pliny, conferred the power of divination.

Esbat: A weekly meeting of covens.

Estrie: A mediaeval demon or witch, capable of changing shape at will. It flies about at night on evil missions, and drinks human blood like a vampire.

Evil Eye: A term used of the malefic potency, to the point of death, believed to be inherent in the glance of certain persons, in "fiery and baleful eyes," as the Malleus Maleficarum asserts. In ancient Assyria, the evil eye could be exorcised by spells and incantations. Among the Romans, the belief in fascinatio—the Latin term for the evil eye— was widespread. The poet Persius, in his second satire, refers to the tying of multi-colored threads on the necks of infants, to ward off fascinatio. Pliny the Elder suggests spittle as an antidote. In later times, a fleur-de-lis design was used as an amulet for the same purpose.

The belief is still common in Italy, where it is called mal d'occhio. In the South, especially in Naples, it is known as jettatura. In Corsica, the peasants have a deep fear of innochiatura. In general, along the Mediterranean littoral, and in Arabia, the evil eye is a reality.

In Iran, nazar means a spell cast by an evil eye. To ward off the evil eye, Moslems say: Ma sha'llah (What God wills). Suras recited from the Koran are also recited for the same apotropaic purpose.

In Scotland, the expression "struck" or "overlooked" was used to indicate cattle affected by the evil eye. In Irish folklore, the evil eye is still called "the eye of Balor." (See: Balor). In Irish demonology, moreover, eye-biting witches were so described on account of their ability to cast a spell by means of the evil eye.

Excrement: Human and animal excrement was a common ingredient in magic potions and also for therapeutic purposes. In particular demand was the excrement of the dog, wolf, ox, cow, pig, goat, sheep, pigeon, goose, hen, and mice.

Execution: The last execution for witchcraft took place in 1722, in Scotland.

Exorcism: The expulsion of evil spirits or demons from persons or places by means of occult rites involving spells, incantations, and conjurations. One method, employed in the case of Sarah, a Median princess possessed by the demon Asmodeus, was to mix incense with heart and liver of fish and to set the mixture on fire, the smoke fumes routing the demon from the victim's body.

In his Antiquities of the Jews, Book 8, the historian Josephus mentions a certain Eleazar, a Jew, who exorcised a demon in the presence of the Emperor Vespasian:

"Eleazar put a ring that had a root of one of those sorts mentioned by Solomon to the nostrils of the demoniac, after which he drew out the demon through his nostrils: and when the man fell down, immediately he abjured him to return into him no more, still making mention of Solomon, and reciting the incantation which he composed. And when Eleazar would persuade and demonstrate to the spectators that he had such a power, he set a little way off a cup or basin full of water, and commanded the demon as he went out of the man to overturn it, and thereby to let the spectators know that he had left the man. And when this was done, the skill and wisdom of Solomon was shown very manifestly."

The Vedas, the sacred books of Hindu literature, contain magical prayers used as forms of exorcism.

Eye of Horus: An Egyptian charm worn around the neck as a protection against evil forces.

F

Familiar: An attendant demon attached to a witch or wizard, sometimes assuming the form of a cat, dog, mole, spider, rat, ape, hare, toad, or ferret. These familiars had names such as Swein, Zequiel, Rory, Robin. In France, popular names were: Volon, Phrin, Rago, Rapha. Pet names in England included dandriprat, little master, bunn, naumet, puckril.

The witch could acquire a familiar by performing certain magic rites involving the desecration of the Host.

The magician Agrippa had a familiar in the shape of a black dog, called Monsieur. Another familiar was Josaphat, who attended Jehanneret Regnal-le-Boiteux, a French fifteenth century wizard. Oliver Cromwell, who is reputed to have dabbled in Black Magic, had a familiar named Grimoald.

In Malayan sorcery, each pawang or magician has a familiar that is a hereditary spirit, acquired and bequeathed through successive generations.

Fapisia: In Portuguese legend, a herb that drives away demons.

Fattura della Morte: The death-maker. An Italian device used in sympathetic magic. A lemon, stuck with nails, is smoked over a fire to the accompaniment of incantations.

Feather: In Egyptian magic, a feather was the symbol of truth.

Fetishism: In the field of magic, worship of objects in which powerful spirits are assumed to reside.

Fingers: In Turkish legend, one ate with the first three fingers only, because the devil ate with the other two.

Finskgalden: In Icelandic magic practice, the domination and mastery of a demon, who follows the sorcerer in the form of a worm or fly and helps him to perform thaumaturgy.

Fish: Fish were usual offerings to demons and other infernal powers. A triglé, a kind of fish, was a frequent sacrifice to Hecate.

Fong-Onhang: In Chinese occult legend, a fabulous bird, similar to the phoenix.

Formulae of invocation: An ancient formula for invoking demons runs thus:

Xilka, Xilka, Besa, Besa.

Another was as follows:

Bagahi laca Bachabé.

Also:

Palas aron azinomas.

Fortune-tellers: An ancient branch of fortune-telling consisted of actually selling ready-made fortunes. Dreams involved personal futures, and were also for sale. Juvenal, the Roman satirist of the second century A.D., describes the Appian Way as swarming with Jewish fortune-tellers who sell dreams at a cheap rate.

Fragarach: In Irish legend, a sword endowed with magic properties.

Francis Barrett: An early nineteenth century professor of Chemistry in London, who lectured on the Kabala and on magic. He also gave private instruction in the occult arts. In 1801 he published The Magus, in which he describes, on a comprehensive scale, the characteristics of demons, conjurations and spells, necromancy and all other related phases of goety.

Fredegonde: A Frankish Queen of the sixth century, who was reputedly endowed with the Evil Eye and also practiced sorcery.

G

Gandreid: In Icelandic magic, an operation that effects transvection by air.

Garlic: A charm against the evil eye and assaults by vampires.

Garter: Among witches, the wearing of a garter was a badge of rank.

Gastromancy: Divination by ventriloquial operation.

Gello: In ancient Greek legend, a kind of female vampire or goblin that carried off young children. The gello is mentioned by Sappho in one of her poems, and is also known in modern Greek folklore.

Geloscopy: Divination by observing a person's laughter.

Gematria: A Kabalistic cryptogrammatic method, based on the twenty-two letters of the Hebrew alphabet, used to discover the numerical values of the letters and hence the relationship between words.

Geomancy: A method of divination of the future by an examination of handfuls of earth.

George Ripley: An English alchemist and occultist of the fifteenth century who was said to have transmuted base metal into gold.

George Sinclair (1654-1696): A Scottish professor of philosophy and mathematics who wrote a book on witchcraft entitled Satan's Invisible World Discovered.

Georgius Sabellicus: A famous fifteenth century magician and necromancer.

Ghirlanda della Streghe: Witch's Garland. Among Italian witches, this object was used in sympathetic magic. It consisted of a series of knots, with the feathers of a black hen stuck in them at intervals. An incantation was said over the garland.

Ghost: A disembodied spirit: also called a spectre, phantom, apparition.

Ghoul: In Arab demonology, a fiend with one eye, wings, and an animal shape, often flesh-devouring.

Giacomo Casanova (1725-1798): An Italian adventurer in whose life magic practices played a dominant role. He invented a cryptogram, called a "kabbala," that he used in divination. He possessed, among other works, the Key of Solomon and a book on the conjuration of demons, and hence became involved with the Inquisition. In his contacts with European society he participated in occult treasure hunts and the conjuration of gnomes.

Gibel-Nusku: The efficacy of wax images was anciently destroyed by repeating this powerful name.

Gilles de Rais (1404-1440): A French nobleman who, after squandering a vast fortune, resorted to necromantic practices, with the aid of sorcerer-associates, to retrieve his wealth. For his occult practices he was put to death.

Gilles Garnier: A sixteenth century Frenchman, of Lyons, who was condemned to be burnt alive on a charge of lycanthropy.

Giovanni Battista della Porta (1538-1615): A Neapolitan physicist interested in magic. As a young man, he published his Natural Magic, which was later, in 1589, published again, in expanded form, in twenty books. He also founded in Naples an Academy of the Secrets of Nature. Natural Magic deals with a variety of subjects, including perfumes, but the most significant chapters, in relation to the occult arts, are those on the transmutation of metals.

Glosopetra: A magic stone, said to have fallen from Heaven during a waning moon. Shaped like a human tongue, it was used by magicians.

Gnostics: Adherents of Gnosticism, a doctrine that embraced features of the Babylonian, Egyptian, Persian, and Christian religions, the Hebraic mystic Kabala, and the magic arts. The Gnostics based their spiritual salvation on the totality of their secret knowledge and on magic practices, and for long periods were considered fundamentally as sorcerers.

Goat without horns: In Voodoo, a human being—intended for sacrifice.

Goblin: A mischievous demon.

Goetia (Goety): A term, derived from Greek, meaning witchcraft.

Golden Disc: The Golden Disc of the Four Castles: a magic disc, once the property of Dr. John Dee and now in the British Museum.

Golem: In Hebraic legend, a monstrous automaton endowed with life by magical means. The formula for creating a golem, left by a certain Eleazar of Worms in Germany, in the thirteenth century, was to secure virgin soil from a mountain spot untrod by man. Over each organ of the golem the mystic alphabets of the 221 gates were to be chanted, while the Divine Name must be incised on the forehead of the creature.

Throughout Hebraic history many such robots have appeared. The sixteenth century Kabalist Elijah of Chelm made an android, which became alive when the mystic divine name was written on the automaton's forehead. But the most famous Golem was produced by Rabbi Judah Loew of Prague in the late sixteenth century. This Golem served his master by protecting the welfare of the Jews. Fearful, however, of possible desecration of the Sabbath by the Golem, every Sabbath eve the Rabbi removed the life-principle, which he had injected into the Golem with the help of a magic formula.

Graeco-Egyptian Magic: In certain Greek papyri, found in Egypt and belonging to the first and second century A.D., the magic techniques for securing favors from spirits, demons, and the gods of the Underworld are presented in detail. The prescriptions include the making of wax images for love-spells, the use of amulets, animal sacrifices, awesome invocations and conjurations.

An exorcism in which Selene, the Moon Goddess, is invoked, requires the use of crusts of bread, coral, turtle-dove blood, a hair from a virgin ox, a camel hoof, colt's foot, a female corpse, and the genitals of a monkey.

Gram: In Nordic legend, a sword that possessed magical properties.

Grand Copt: A title assumed by Cagliostro, under which title he claimed to have lived, by means of an occult prescription, through successive centuries.

Grandier: Urbain Grandier was a priest of Loudun in France, who was accused of bewitching the local nuns. Arrested on a charge of sorcery, he was tortured and burned alive in 1634. His pact with the Devil is preserved in the Bibliothèque Nationale.

Gratoulet: A famous French sorcerer of the sixteenth century.

Greal: In Celtic mythology, a magic drink that induces inspiration.

Greece (belief in magic): Magic and the supernatural elements associated with its operations were a matter of intense belief among the early Greek cosmologists and the pre-Socratic philosophers. Thales and Heraclitus in the sixth century B.C. believed in the magic circle. To Thales demons were real. Later, even Plato accepted the existence of ghosts, spirits of the dead returned to this world. He also alluded, in his philosophical dialogues, to magic knots, enchantments, and divination from the entrails of animals. At the hour of death, he declared, men possessed the power of prophecy.

According to Porphyry, a Greek philosopher of the third century A.D., there were demons who haunted homes and harassed the occupants.

Many Greek writers of comedy, from Aristophanes to Menander, frequently allude to magic practices.

Grimoire: A magician's manual.

Guibourg: The sinister Abbé Guibourg participated in magic rites associated with Madame de Montespan and was executed.

Guido Bonatti: A thirteenth century Italian astrologer and magician. On one occasion he brought wealth to an apothecary friend by making a wax image of a magically endowed ship.

Guillaume de Paris: A mediaeval wizard who made statues that could speak, with demoniac agency.

Guillaume de Postel (1510-1581): A French Kabalist and astrologer. The son of poor peasants, he succeeded in becoming a master of Oriental languages, engaged in diplomatic missions, and was later appointed professor of Oriental languages and mathematics.

He gave up his position, however, and traveled and lectured. Claiming to have received revelation in the stars, he adapted certain Gnostic beliefs, asserting that the male and female principles were incorporated in himself. Imprisoned by the Inquisition, he escaped, and finally returned to his professorship in Paris. His lectures, however, full of mysticism, compelled him to flee, to a convent, where he spent the rest of his life.

He wrote The Key of Things Kept Secret from the Foundation of the World.

Gyromancy: Divination by walking round a chalked circle and noting the position of the body in relation to the circle.

H

Hag-stones: So called in England, and known as mare-stones in Scotland. They were bored stones worn as amulets to avert nightmare.

Hair: When making a compact with Satan, the witch offers her hair, that Satan makes into hail. It was believed that magic potency resided in hair: hence witches were shorn clean, in the Middle Ages, before torture.

Hamon: A magic stone, like gold, and shaped like a ram's horn. It was used as a medium of revelation of divine mysteries.

Hand of Glory: The hand cut off from a felon who has been hanged on a gibbet. Such a hand, dried and steeped in various salts, was used in spells.

Hanon—Tramp: In Teutonic lore, a nightmare demon.

Hantu Kubor: In Malayan magic, grave demons. These are spirits of the dead that prey on the living.

Hantu Pusaka: A Malayan demon.

Harry Houdini (originally Harry Weiss) (1874-1926). A professional magician who performed amazing feats of escape that he admitted were not beyond his personal control. He acquired, however, a global reputation for performing feats beyond normal explanation, and still unsolvable. During his lifetime he was passionately interested in the history of his work, and accumulated a rare and comprehensive library of books on magic, now in the Library of Congress. During the latter part of his life Houdini devoted himself to exposing alleged spiritualists who claimed communication with the dead.

Head of Baphomet: Such heads of spirits were worshipped by the Gnostics as a divinity. Later on, they were equally revered by The Templars.

Hecate: A triple goddess, patroness of witchcraft in ancient Greek and Roman mythology. She is first mentioned by the ancient Greek poet Hesiod. She is accompanied by souls of the dead, and dogs howl at her nocturnal approach.

Heinrich Khunrath: A German physician and alchemist of the sixteenth century.

Heka: A primordial Egyptian god, whose name also means "magic."

Hekakontalithos: A magic stone that was used by the Troglodites, in occult rites, as an offering to the demons.

Hekau: An Egyptian term for the magic words inscribed on an amulet.

Heliotrope: A magic herb reputed to confer invisibility.

Hellawes: In Arthurian legend, a notorious sorcerer.

Hepatoscopy: Divination by examining a sheep's liver.

Herbs: Herbs that were considered efficacious in banishing sickness, discovering stolen property, exorcising haunted cattle, diverting witchcraft, understanding bird language, rendering oneself invisible, included: forest manna, sage, meadow mint, alsine pubescens, symplocarpus, Eben herbs, teriac, rue, orris root, lungwort, St. Peter's root, suntull, wormwood, enzian, veronica, malaxis, centifolium, christianwort.

Hermes Chthonios: A Greek deity identified in Egypt with Thoth.

Hermes Trismegistus: Hermes three times the Greatest. A name of the Egyptian god Thoth, master of alchemical knowledge. He was the reputed originator of treatises on magic, alchemy, and astrology.

Hermetic: One who practices alchemy or occult arts.

Hexagram: A six-pointed figure, called the Shield of David, that was used in magic rites, particularly to control demons.

Hexenhaus: The House of the Witches, in Bamberg, Germany. It was built expressly and used in the seventeenth century as a kind of court in which witches were brought to trial.

Hijab: Among Arabs, an amulet or charm used to ward off

bad luck or win favor. A popular amulet is in the form of a hand.

Hippomancy: Divination by observing a horse's pace.

Hippomanes: A growth said to be found on the forehead of newborn foals: used in love-philtres in ancient times.

Hobgoblin: A mischievous spirit, that plays pranks on human beings.

Holda: Among the ancient Gauls, a kind of nocturnal Sabbat at which magicians participated in orgies with demons transformed into dancing women.

Home of Magic: In Celtic legend, the homes of magic were submarine regions known as Lochlann and Sorcha, inhabited by spirits called Fomorians. Their chief was one-eyed Balor.

Homer: The earliest Greek writer whose work has been preserved. In his epic poems the Iliad and especially the Odyssey he describes many magic practices. In the Odyssey an incantation is chanted to stop the flow of blood of the wounded hero Odysseus. Circe, the siren who lures Odysseus, uses potions, a magic wand, and ointments in producing transformations of men into animals. She also has the power of exorcism and teaches Odysseus to summon the spirits of the dead from the Other World.

Horse: In mediaeval legend the Devil and his demons often took the form of a horse. A coltpixie, for instance, was a malevolent spirit, in equine form, that lured real horses to destruction in swamps.

Wizards and necromancers employed such horses in their sinister practices. Bayard was the demon horse, brought from Hell, of the necromancer Malagigi.

Among the Saxons the horse was credited with occult powers. According to the Roman historian Tacitus the Germanic tribes practiced divination by observation of the whinnying and neighing of certain sacred horses.

Horse shoes: In the Middle Ages, horse shoes were nailed to the threshold to exclude witches.

Houmfort: A voodoo temple.

Hounga: Another name for a Pappaloi.

Hu-Jum-Sin: A Chinese occultist who practiced alchemy.

Hydromancy: A means of discovering hidden objects by gazing into water surfaces.

Hyena: A stone whose possessor could foretell the future.

Hypocephalus: An Egyptian amulet in the form of a bronze disc or of linen, inscribed with magic symbols.

I

Iamblicus: A Neo-Platonist philosopher (250-325 A.D.) who wrote a defense of magic entitled The Mysteries of the Egyptians, Chaldeans, and Assyrians, that is still extant.
Iannes and Iambres: Two magicians at the court of Pharaoh who contended with Moses' magic skill. According to Arab legend, two of the magicians who challenged Moses were Sadur and Ghadur.
Iatromancy: Divination, in respect of a probable cure, by means of incubation.
Iblis: In Iranian demonology, a term for Satan.
Ichthyomancy: Divination by the inspection of the entrails of fish.
Idris: A Welsh magician-giant. Geographically, his name is commemorated in Cader Idris—the Chair of Idris: a hollow area on a Welsh mountain-peak.
Image Magic (also known as Sympathetic Magic): A means of injuring or destroying an enemy by harming an image fashioned into the likeness of the victim. The effigy was made of wax or clay or other plastic material. In ancient Assyria, wood, wool, bitumen, tallow were also used. The Egyptians of the Old Kingdom used wax. There is testimony in papyri of the third dynasty, about 3800 B.C., of a crocodile made of wax, intended to devour an enemy.

The image was punctured with pins, thorns, or needles, or flint darts were thrown at the figure, or some similar mutilation was performed. Correspondingly, the melting of the image caused dissolution of the original. This ancient device was known as early as the reign of Rameses III, in the twelfth century B.C. In an Assyrian cuneiform tablet there is reference to an image made of a witch. The device was also in use among the Greeks and the Romans and in the Middle East. In the Greek poet Theocritus the sorcerer kills his enemies by magic rites performed over an effigy of the victim. Similar effigies are described in the bucolic poems of the Roman poet Vergil. Images called "pictures" were known to Celtic witches. Later, in Scotland, these images were called "clay bodies."

Many cases in history attest the prevalence of the practice. In the seventh century a certain Scottish King Duffus had his wax image roasted and melted by a company of witches bent on his destruction. In 1066 the Jews of Trèves were accused of making such an image of a certain Bishop Eberhard. In 1560 a wax image of Queen Elizabeth of England, with a pin stuck in the breast, was found in London. The practice is still in force, among primitive tribes and also in putatively enlightened areas. Within living memory, images have been discovered in the North of Scotland, in brooks, on hillsides, and in fields. In World War II numberless images of Hitler were subjected to sympathetic magic. In Malaya, the making of wax images is a common feature of wizardry.

Imaguncula: The Latin term for the image used in sympathetic magic.

Incantation: A magic formula, usually whispered to increase efficacy and incomprehensibility, used to bewitch a person, summon demons, or perform similar acts. In the Metamorphoses, Apuleius uses the phrase "with magic whispering." On occasion the formula may be written on fruit or leaves, imbibed with liquids, or soaked in honey.

In the seventh century B.C. Assurbanipal, King of Assyria, appeals to the star-god Sirius to "take away the enchantment" by which he is beset.

A typical Chaldean incantation, involving sympathetic magic, the casting of spells, and the evil eye, runs as follows:

He who forges the image, he who enchants—
The spiteful face, the evil eye,
The mischievous mouth, the mischievous tongue,
The mischievous lips, the mischievous words,

Spirit of the Sky, remember!
Spirit of the Earth, remember!
An Assyrian exorcism, recited over sick people, runs
thus:
The man of Ea am I,
The man of Damkina am I,
The messenger of Marduk am I,
My spell is the spell of Ea,
My incantation is the incantation of Marduk,
The circle of Ea is in my hand,
The tamarisk, the powerful weapon of Anu,
In my hand I hold,
The date—spathe, mighty in decision,
In my hand I hold.

In the eighth eclogue, a pastoral poem by the Roman
poet Vergil, there is a description of a Thessalian girl who
performs magic rites and makes wax figurines in order to
bring back her lover Daphnis.

In the 1930's, among the natives of Dobu, a South Sea
Island, incantations were still used in connection with
theft and adultery, and also to produce disease.

Incense: Incense was used in exorcisms to help spirits to
materialize.

In Malayan magic, different incenses were used for different demons. Such incenses, or ingredients included:
euphorbia, bdellium, ammoniac, brains of a raven, sul-
phur, human blood, blood of a black cat.

A Malayan invocation to the Spirit of Incense, which is
a potent factor in magical rites, runs as follows:
Zabur Hijau is your name, O incense,
Zabur Bajang the name of your Mother,
Zabur Puteh the name of your Fumes.

May you fumigate the Seven Tiers of the Earth,
May you fumigate the Seven Tiers of the Sky
And serve as a summons to all spirits,
To those that have magic power.

Incubus: A demon that copulates with women.

Infernal Monarchy: According to the demonographer Weirus, the hierarchy of the Infernal Regions is arranged thus:

One Emperor
Seven Kings
Twenty-four Dukes
Thirteen demons who hold the rank of marquis
Ten Counts
Eleven Presidents.

Influence of witchcraft: Witchcraft, operating in devious ways, manifests itself in a variety of circumstances. Loneliness is a factor susceptible to its potency. Among the natives of Dobu, a South Sea island, a person wandering alone in the bush is in constant danger of witchcraft.

Invisibility: A manuscript in the Bibliothèque de l'Arsenal de Paris contains a long prayer, in Latin, whose recital promises invisibility. The prayer invokes Pontation, Master of Invisibility, along with the names of some sixty demons.

Isaac of Holland: A fifteenth century alchemist.

Isle of Man: An island off the West coast of England that was one of the chief centres of ancient Druidism.

Isobel Gowdie: A seventeenth century Scottish witch, of Auldearne. She bore the Devil's Mark on her shoulder.

Iwangis: Sorcerers of the Molucca Islands, reputed to devour dead bodies.

J

Jacques Gafferel (1601-1681): A magician employed as librarian to Cardinal Richelieu.

Jadi-jadian: In Malayan legend, a person capable of changing into a tiger: a were-tiger, similar to a werewolf.

Jammabos: Japanese magicians who claim converse with Satan and also the power to resuscitate the dead.

Jeannette Biscar: A sorceress whom the devil, in goat form, carried to a Sabbat.

Jechiel: Rabbi Jechiel, a Kabalist and physician who lived in the reign of St. Louis of France, had a magic lamp that needed no replenishment and a nail that struck burning agony into his enemies.

Jigar-Khor: In Hindu demonology, a liver-eater, a sorcerer.

Johann Georg Schröpfer (1730-1774): a German necromancer who acquired a wide and awesome reputation in Leipzig and throughout Germany. He practiced witchcraft against his enemies, initiated many disciples, but died a suicide.

John Lambe: Dr. John Lambe was an English wizard who, among other activities, practiced prognostication. One of his adherents was said to be the Duke of Buckingham. Lambe was stoned to death by a London mob in 1628.

Joseph Glanvil (1636-1680): An English divine who published in 1668 a book on witchcraft.

Julianus: Called Theurgus, the Necromancer. He once drove out a plague from Rome by magical power.

Julius Firmicus Maternus: A Roman of the fourth century A.D. who wrote an elaborate treatise, in eight books, on astrology and magic.

K

Kabala: A body of mystic Hebraic lore, dealing largely with spirits and demons and methods of controlling them. One branch of Kabala deals with mystic operations involving anagrams, names of spirits and angels and other occult matters revealed through calculations, "perscrutations," and permutations of words and numbers.

According to the Kabala, all men are endowed with magical powers that they themselves may develop.

Kamlat: Among the Tartars of Siberia, a magic technique of conjuring demons with drums.

Kang-Hi: In Chinese demonology, lord of the Infernal Regions.

Kannas (also called **Quobdas**): A sorcerer's kettle drum, used for enchantments among Laplanders.

Karina: In Egyptian demonology, a familiar, attached to each child at birth.

Katakhanes: In the demonology of Ceylon, a vampire.

Key of Solomon the King: A book on magic putatively ascribed to King Solomon, but actually of mediaeval origin. It was one of the most popular treatises in the Middle Ages. The contents covered instructions on how to summon demons, requirements of the performing magician in respect of dress, perfumes, fire, instruments, and details on constructing the magic circle.

Khamuas: The son of Rameses the Second. An Egyptian magician.

Kishuph: A Hebraic term meaning witchcraft: used in the Kabala.

Knights Templar: A mediaeval organization composed of knights, farmers, and men in holy orders, who were under Cistercian-reformed Benedictine rule. Early in the fourteenth century they were prosecuted as Satanists.

Knot: Knots were so frequently associated with magic rites, especially in sympathetic magic, that "binding" or "tying knots" was another term for magic in general. Knots—whether of multicolored threads, plant stems, animal hair—were used generally to remove a spell, or to cure headache, fever, ophthalmia. The knot design was common in Egyptian talismans. Petronius, the Roman novelist who flourished in Nero's reign, mentions, in his Satyricon 131, a witch who took from her bosom a web of multicolored twisted threads and bound it to the neck of one of the characters in the tale, to free him from a spell.

Kobold: A mediaeval demon, in the form of a homunculus, that mimicked the human voice. The kobold was a familiar of ventriloquists.

Koran: Among Moslems, the Koran is used in bibliomancy. This procedure is called istikhara, "cutting the Koran."

Kosh: An African forest demon.

Kurds: The Kurds of Kurdistan are reputed to be Devil-worshippers.

L

La Broosha: An alternate Spanish form of Lilith, often taking the shape of a cat.

Lacnunga: A medico-magical mediaeval text that deals with herbal remedies and magic chants.

Lamia: A demon who stole children and sucked their blood. She was known to the ancient Greeks, who considered the lamia bisexual.

Lampadomancy: Divination by means of the flame of a lamp.

Lapis Iudaicus: The Jewish Stone. A mystic stone, also called Theolithos, or Lapis Exilis.

Last Witch: Alice Molland, found guilty of using spells to exterminate three persons, was the last witch in England to be executed, in 1685.

Laws against witchcraft: The Old Testament forbids the practice of magic:

Thou shalt not suffer a witch to live: Exodus 22.18.

An edict against wizards and witches was also promulgated by Saul.

Leviticus 20.27 enjoins death on anyone having a familiar spirit or on a wizard.

Likewise, Deuteronomy 18.10-12 inveighs against enchanters, astrologers, witches, and necromancers.

In ancient Egypt, Greece, and Rome, magicians were prosecuted, and magic was outlawed, with the imposition of severe penalties. Plato, the Greek philosopher, enjoined punishment for the abuse of witchcraft. The Romans too took measures to control wizardry. In the fifth century B.C. The Twelve Tables forbade magical rites. The Romans set up a Council of Ten to punish sorcerers. In 139 B.C. the Roman praetor ordered all thaumaturgists to leave Rome and Italy within ten days. But they kept on returning to the capital. In 96 B.C. human sacrifices in magic rites were forbidden by law in Rome. Toward the end of the Republic, M. Vipsanius Agrippa, a prominent magistrate, found the city again swarming with magicians, and banished them. The Emperor Augustus ordered all books on magic to be burned publicly. In Tiberius' reign magicians were exiled. In succeeding reigns, as late as the second century A.D., decrees were issued against astrologers and seers and those who consulted them. Again, Constantius, Valentinian I, and Valens made divination, astrology, and magic a political crime. Constantius actually made the consultation of a seer, diviner, or magician an offense punishable by death. On the other hand, certain Roman Emperors participated in magic practices: among them Commodus, Caracalla, and Julian the Apostate. Alexander Severus, in the third century A.D., consulted wizards and even subsidized them with salaries, but publicly he approved punishment, of exile or a fine, in the case of men found in possession of books on magic. In the fourth and fifth century, again, legislation condemned the cultivation of the goetic arts. In 385 A.D. the Emperor Theodosius prohibited magic sacrifices under penalty of death.

The Salic Laws, enacted in the fifth century, fined any person who associated with vampires for the purpose of enchantments. A slightly larger fine was imposed on vampires guilty of anthropophagism.

During the fourteenth century, on several successive occasions, laws were promulgated by Church and secular authorities against witchcraft, which was treated as a religious heresy.

In Henry VIII's reign, in 1542, an Act was passed against "conjurations and witchcrafts and sorcery and enchantments."

In 1563, in Queen Elizabeth's reign, a Bill was passed against witchcraft, imposing penalties in the ratio of the seriousness of the wizardry. Another Act against witchcraft, passed in England in 1604, in the reign of James I of England, was directed against "conjuration, witchcraft and dealing with evil and wicked spirits." Under its provisions some 70,000 witches, according to one estimate, were put to death. The severity of punishment against Black Magic was further confirmed by an Act of 1604 and another one of 1649.

Lecanomancy: Divination by means of dropping precious stones into water and listening to the resultant sound.

Lemegeton: Also called The Lesser Key of Solomon. The name itself is of obscure, undetermined origin. It is a mediaeval manuscript, now in the British Museum, containing lists of the seventy-two demons in hierarchical progression. These spirits, once rebellious angels, are not, however, always malevolent. They teach astrology and geomancy, languages, herbal secrets, and necromancy. They confer invisibility and the faculty of rapid transportation and the power of transformation, but also they effect storms, ruin, earthquakes, and other cataclysmic phenomena.

Lemures: Among the Romans, nocturnal ghosts that sometimes entered homes and could be expelled by throwing beans.

Levitation: The raising of the body, or of inanimate objects, into the air, contrary to the laws of gravitation. There is on record the case of an Italian monk, St. Joseph of Copertino, who in the seventeenth century flew by auto-levitation from the middle of a church to the tabernacle of the high altar, a distance of forty feet.

This power of levitation or transvection through the air is recorded historically in official investigations of witches. It is also attributed to certain Tibetan priests.

Libanius: A magician who, during the siege of Ravenna by the Emperor Constantius, used magical means to overpower the enemy.

Libanomancy: Divination by means of incense smoke.

Liber Spirituum: The Book of Spirits. A mediaeval manual of black magic.

Libo Drusus: A Roman magician and necromancer mentioned by the historian Tacitus in his Annales.

Lilith: A female demon, associated with Assyrian demonology. According to a Talmudic legend, she was Adam's first wife, and bore him demons. She was represented as having wings and appearing with hair dishevelled.

Lindheim: In Lindheim, Germany, there is a structure called The Tower of the Witches, reputed to have been the meeting place of witches in the Middle Ages.

Lithomancy: Divination by means of precious stones.

Little Albert: A famous Black Magic book or grimoire that gives directions for summoning spirits by means of magic circles and other figures.

Lotapes: An ancient magician, associated with Pharaoh's court.

Louis Eugène Flaque: A French sorcerer and Kabalist of the nineteenth century.

Louis Gaufridi: A wizard, known as the Prince of Sorcerers, who was executed in 1611.

Loup-garou: A French term for a werewolf.

Lubin: A fish, whose heart can drive off demons.

Lucifer: A variant name for Satan. As the "Light-bearer," he has his home in the East. Dante describes him as having three heads and six wings, around which the Fiend's activities revolve.

Luciferians: Mediaeval Satanists who flourished in the thirteenth century, and worshipped and sacrificed to demons at midnight ceremonies.

Lucifuge Rofocale: The arch demon in the Grand Grimoire, Prime Minister to Lucifer.

Lycanthropy: The changing of human beings into wolves. (See Werewolf.) Circe, the witch in Homer's Odyssey, changed men into wolves. Plato refers to the practice.

Pliny the Elder, in his encyclopedic Historia Naturalis, mentions a family one of whose members, in each generation, became a wolf for nine years.

Other ancient writers who testify to the prevalence of

lycanthropy include Varro, Vergil, Strabo, Pomponius Mela, and Solinus.

In the sixteenth century in France edicts were issued against warlocks who practiced lycanthropy.

Similar to lycanthropy is the belief in the were-tiger, prevalent in Malayan magic. In Africa, the belief is that men change into hyenas and tigers; in Iceland, into bears; in India, into leopards and tigers.

M

Macionica: In Slavonic demonology, a witch.

Madame de Montespan: One of the mistresses of Louis XIV of France who, in order to retain the king's affection, practiced magical arts, participating in an Amatory Mass, the concoction of love-philtres, and child sacrifice. She died, however, in repentance and sanctity.

Associated with her was the witch La Voisin, Lesage, an alchemist, and the sinister Abbé Guibourg.

Madeleine Amalaric: A French witch of the sixteenth century, who was put to death as being instrumental in the death of eleven persons.

Madeleine Bavan: A seventeenth century sorceress, notorious for her activities at the Sabbat.

Magia Naturalis et Innaturalis: A book on magic, subtitled The Three-fold Harrowing of Hell, written by Dr. Johannes Faustus and current in mediaeval Germany.

Magic: Magic is an elusive term to define. It is, in a formal sense, the operation of phenomena in so unusual and inexplicable a manner as to induce a belief that the operation is attributable to unknown forces beyond normal power of man, or to such forces subjected, by not normally and readily discernible means, to human power.

A simple and essentially valid definition comes from an old Latin declamation, erroneously attributed to Quintilian, which states: Magic is the art of going against nature.

Martin Delrio, in his Disquisitionum Magicarum Libri Sex, 1599, defines magic in a virtually similar manner:

> An art or skill which, by means of a not supernatural force, produces certain strange and unusual phenomena whose rationale eludes common sense.

The anthropologist Tylor defines magic as an occult science—which is implicitly a petitio principii—with two branches, spiritistic and natural. Other authorities equate magic with a mystic force or essence issuing from a source of secret power. Lewis Spence postulates a supplementary definition, suggesting that magic is a power, latent in human beings, of controlling cosmic matter by their will and faith.

Magic Candle: A candle, made of the fat of a hanged criminal, that was used in conjunction with the Hand of Glory as a means of discovering hidden treasure.

Magic Circle: A circle drawn around a person or an object that was to be subjected to the operation of magic. The circle, described with a new sword around the sorcerer who was to invoke a demon, symbolized the boundary that separated the demon from the magician. In the first century A.D. a certain Honi Ha Me'agel, a Hebraic thaumaturgist, produced rain from heaven, while standing within such a circle. His success was so frequent that he was nicknamed the circle-drawer.

The magic circle was also used as a protective measure for warding off evil spirits. In ancient Assyria a sick man was safeguarded against the onslaught of fiends by being placed in an enchanted circle of flour. In ancient India, too, a circle of black pebbles was used by the magician to safeguard a woman at childbirth against demons. In the Middle Ages the protective circle was normally used by the practicing magician.

Magic formulae: The following magic formulae, deriving from the writings of Albertus Magnus, were in common use in the Middle Ages as means of banishing various forms of sickness or in other emergencies:

> Ofano, Oblamo, Ospergo.
> Hola Noa Massa.
> Light, Beff, Cletemati, Adonai,
> Cleona, Florit.
> Pax Sax Sarax.
> Afa Afca Nostra.
> Cerum, Heaium, Lada Frium.

Magic in the Bible: Sorcery of all kinds was prevalent in Biblical times, and the Old Testament in particular reflects that condition. This magic, however, was not specifically Jewish, but stemmed from Babylonian and Egyptian sources.

Sorcerers were publicly stoned to death. Trial by ordeal is mentioned in Numbers 5.11-13. A witch—mekashephah in the Hebrew version—is mentioned in Exodus 22.18. The waters of Marah were made sweet by casting in a tree: Exodus 15.25. Moses had a wand that produced water from rocks: Exodus 17.6; and he could also turn the wand into a serpent. Elijah was able to bring down and avert rain. The witch called the witch of Endor could exorcise spirits, while Miriam was healed of leprosy by incantations. As part of his equipment, the High Priest of the Israelites wore the Urim and Thummim, two objects that had an oracular function. In Isaiah 19.3 reference is made to familiar spirits and wizards. In Isaiah 47.12-13 there is an allusion to enchantments, sorceries, astrologers, prognostication. King Manasseh "used enchantments and dealt with familiar spirits and wizards": II Kings 21.6. In II Chronicles 33.6 there is again reference to divination, oracles, and witchcraft. In Acts 16.16, while Paul was at Philippi, "a certain damsel possessed with a spirit of divination met us." Strolling Jews, exorcists, are mentioned in Acts 19.13.

Various passages of the Old Testament—including the Psalms, Genesis, Ezekiel, Deuteronomy, and Proverbs—were often used by mediaeval Jews in the form of recitals or inscriptions, as cures for sickness, as a means of causing the death of an enemy, driving off demons, averting attacks by brigands, winning a war, or becoming invisible.

Malleus Maleficarum: The Witches' Hammer. The title of a Latin treatise on magic by Heinrich Kramer and Jacob Sprenger, Dominicans. It was published in the fifteenth century, and formed the Church basis for investigation and punishment of adepts in witchcraft. The book contains rules for detecting such adepts, and implies that Satan has sanction for his evil operations.

Malphas: An arch-demon of the Infernal Regions.

Mamaloi: A priestess-magician associated with voodooism in the West Indies.

Mambu: Another name for a Mamaloi.

Mandrake: A plant—mandragora officinarum—of the potato family—also called mandragore, that often grows in the shape of human limbs. It was frequently used as an ingredient in love-philtres, and is so mentioned in Genesis 30.14-15. It is also called "the plant of Circe" because her witch-brews were infusions of mandrake.

Mara: In Icelandic lore, a female witch who on her nocturnal jaunts used men for locomotion in place of horses or other means.

Mara: In Tantric Buddhism, according to the sacred text of the Lalitavistra, the Devil, who has at his command four legions of creatures with bodies of flame, skins of boars, stags, ichneumons, rams, beetles, cats, apes, wolves; breathing flames, pouring out a rain of brass or molten iron, or black clouds.

Mare: A demon that deprives men of speech during sleep and induces nightmares.

Margaritomancy: Divination by means of a pearl.

Marie Balcoin: A French sorceress in the reign of Henry IV, condemned to the stake for her witchcraft.

Mark: The mark of the witch was a red or blue spot on the body, produced by some tattooing process, that branded the witch as an adherent of Satan. The mark was also known as the Devil's Mark.

Tertullian, one of the Latin Fathers, says it is the Devil's custom to mark his adherents. The mark is "insensible and being pricked it will not bleed," as a certain witch-hunting Richard Bernard advised seventeenth century Grand Jurymen.

Mark Antony Bragadini: A sixteenth century alchemist of

Venice, beheaded for boasting of transmutations with demoniac help.

Marsi: An ancient Italic tribe, according to Pliny the Elder, skilled in sorcery. Marsic magicians were especially known for curing the bites of poisonous snakes.

Martin Delrio: A sixteenth century Spanish prosecutor of sorcerers, who also wrote a book on witchcraft and magicians.

Martines de Pasqually: An eighteenth century Hermetic.

Mary the Jewess: An adept in alchemy who lived in the fourth century A.D. Her name has survived in the modern expression bain-marie, used in chemistry.

Maskim: In Chaldean demonology, the seven maskim were cosmic demons who caused universal destruction.

Mass of St. Secaire: An obscure Satanic Mass said in Basque country and still reputedly conducted in Gascony.

Master John: A necromancer who, in the fourteenth century, was implicated in planning the death of Edward II of England by occult means.

Mathematici: Among the Romans, mathematici were astrologers and diviners, and classed with the Chaldeans, exponents of black magic. The Emperor Diocletian in the third century A.D. forbade the practice of the mathematici.

Mathonwy: In Welsh legend, a ruler of the Underworld and a master of magic.

Matthew Hopkins: A seventeenth century English lawyer who, under the title of Witch-finder General, launched a wide campaign for the extermination of witches. He was responsible for the execution of hundreds—some believe thousands—of victims.

Medea: A witch famous in Greek and Roman mythology: skilled in herbal lore, able to renew youth and make warriors invulnerable. She possesses a box of magic-making drugs. Her powers are well illustrated in the legend of Jason and the Argonauts.

Melampus: An ancient Greek who wrote two works on

divination. He discussed the significance of moles on the human body as a means of such divination.

Membrum Virile: For apotropaic purposes a wooden membrum virile was often used against the Evil Eye.

Menat: An Egyptian amulet possessing magic properties and uniting the male and female principles.

Merlin: A mediaeval wizard who appears prominently in the Arthurian cycle of legends. His parentage was associated with nightmare demons.

Metoposcopy: An occult technique directed toward the evaluation of a person's character and fate from the lines on the forehead.

Mexico: In pre-Columban days the Mexicans had a witch cult, whose queen was represented as riding naked on a broom stick.

Mezuzah: A Hebraic amulet containing the Divine Name, affixed to doorposts of Jewish houses as a protection against demons.

Michael Psellus: A Byzantine polymath of the eleventh century who wrote On the Operation of Demons.

Michael Scot (circa 1175-1232): A Scottish magician. Astrologer at the court of the Emperor Frederick II, Scot wrote numerous books on the occult, describing magic activities in such detail—ranging from necromancy and incantations to alchemy, divination, and dream-interpretations—that in spite of his denial he was himself credited with magic potency. Many legends were current about his skills in sorcery and his amazing exploits achieved through his occult powers. He is even mentioned by Dante.

Molybdomancy: Divination by means of melted lead.

Mopses: A German secret society that was founded on Black Magic practices.

Museum: In Castletown, Isle of Man, England, there is a unique Museum of Magic and Witchcraft, under the directorship of Dr. Gerald B. Gardner, who is himself a member of a still existant witch coven. The Museum contains photographs, figurines, and other objects used in magic operations, along with rooms equipped with the apparatus necessary for the performance of magic rites: pentacles, talismans, wands, magic circles. One room is a careful replica of a witch's cottage, complete with ritual altar.

Myalism (or Mialism): A type of witchcraft practiced in Jamaica and involving converse with the spirits of the dead.

Myomancy: Divination by means of mice.

N

Nabam: A demon whom it is most propitious to conjure on Saturday.

Nambroth: A demon whom it is most propitious to conjure on Tuesday.

Name: As the essence of a person or object mystically rests in the name, the name, especially among primitive peoples, had an occult potency. Thus a person might have two tribal names, only one of which was known publicly. Revelation of the second name, known only to the person bearing it, would put that person into the power of the tribal magician.

The ancient Egyptians similarly had two names, only the lesser one being publicly known, the second name embodying the magical power of the individual.

Narbonne: A region in the south of France, fertile in magic practices during the Middle Ages.

Natsaw: In Burmese demonology, wizards.

Neck-twister: In Hebraic legend, a demon that attacks children.

Necromancy: The evocation of the spirits of the dead: forbidden by the Law of Moses. Saul used this technique through the help of the witch of Endor. It was believed that spirits could be exorcised only during the first year of death. The spirit might be questioned by a direct challenge by name, or indirectly through a skull.

Among the Romans, the necromancers of Etruria, a district of Western Italy, were particularly well known for their necromantic power.

In the third century A.D. Tertullian, one of the outstanding Latin Church Fathers, fulminates against magicians, who conjure spirits and defile the souls of those long since dead, suffocate young boys to induce them to gasp out oracles, and present wonders by means of tricks of jugglers.

Necromantic Bell: A bell described by Girardius, a writer on necromancy in the eighteenth century. The bell was used in invoking the dead.

Nectanebus: An Egyptian king of the fourth century B.C., who was a renowned magician, skilled in divination, astrology, the concoction of philtres, and the casting of runes. By making wax figurines of enemy fleets and of his own forces, and watching their manoeuvres in a bowl of Nile water, he was able in one case to forecast victory for his forces, and in the other case to circumvent imminent disaster by a timely escape.

Necyomancy: Divination by examining the nerves of a corpse.

Nefer amulet: An Egyptian charm, shaped like a musical instrument, reputed to bring good luck.

Nero: At one time he dabbled in Black Magic, but without success, although he was instructed by Tyridates, king of Armenia, himself a magician.

New: The concept of newness is efficacious in magic rites. Hence fresh objects, being uncontaminated, were preferred by magicians. Unused bowls, newly forged weapons, virgin soil had their inherent potency. Spells were engraved with a new knife. Amulets were inscribed on unused parchment. Circles were drawn with a new sword.

Nicholas Flamel: A sixteenth century French alchemist.

Nightmare: In the Middle Ages, nightmares were considered as visitations of evil apparitions, although as early as the second century A.D. the physician Soranus of Ephesus, investigating the phenomenon, concluded that nightmares were due to medico-physiological conditions.

The Greeks called the nightmare spirits Ephialtes. In the Middle Ages, they were known as succubi and incubi. In Germany, the term was Würger, the strangler. The Russians knew them as Kikimara, and the French as cauchemar. In Switzerland, the name became chauchevieille. In the Balkans, the nightmare was a female, flame-winged spirit called Vjeschitza.

Nine Twigs of Woden: A mediaeval chant describing the magical properties of certain herbs.

Nostradamus (1503-1566): Nostradamus, whose French name was Michel de Notre-Dame, was a physician, an astrologer, and a renowned seer. In his famous series of Centuries, poetic predictions, he foretold personal and national events that coincided amazingly with his occult prognostications.

At the court of Catherine de Medici, herself a patron of astrologers and magicians, Nostradamus continued his cryptically worded predictions, one of which concerned himself. Nostradamus had predicted that he would die "near the bed and the bench." He died, at his desk or bench, on July 1, 1566.

Notarikon: A Kabalistic cryptogrammatic method by which magical sentences were formed from words, or new words from mystical combinations of letters.

Noualli: Aztec magicians.

Numbers: The ancients, particularly the Egyptians and the Hebrews, believed in the magical properties and the occult connotations of numbers. Odd numbers were considered lucky; even numbers provoked attacks by demons. Three was an effective number in incantations, often being repeated three times. Similarly, seven, nine—the square of three—, and multiples of these numbers possessed mystic implications.

According to the Pythagoreans, Greek philosophers and mathematicians, the number ten signified Atlas, who upholds the universe. Five represented justice. Primal chaos, declared the sixth century Greek poet Hesiod, is equated with the number one.

O

Ob: A Syrian demon who utters oracles ventriloquially.

Obayifo: An Ashanti term meaning a witch, a vampire. The expression Obi or Obeah, in Jamaican magic, derives from Obayifo.

Obeah (or Obi): A magic cult prevalent in the West Indies, particularly in Jamaica. It is similar to Voodoo and has elements of ophiolatry in its rites and practices. The use of corpses is one of the features of Obeah, which thus associates it with Satanic sorcery.

Obeah stick: In Jamaica, a staff adorned with entwined serpents, or a carving of a human head. Used by Obeah men in magic operations.

Odherir: In Norse mythology, a magic cauldron.

Oeonisticy: Divination by the flight of birds.

Oenothea: A priestess-witch, mentioned by Apuleius.

Oethanes (or Ostanes): During the invasion of Greece by Xerxes, he is said to have introduced magic among the Greeks.

Oinomancy: Divination by means of wine.

Ololygmancy: Divination by the howling of dogs.

Omen sticks: Sticks that, by their position on falling to the ground, aided the Druids in divination.

Omens: Signs and portents that prognosticated the future. Such omens, read and interpreted according to a magic code, involved bodily conditions, natural phenomena, animal life, casting lots, scrutiny of the hand or face, the reading of the Bible, interpretation of the shape of a drop of melted wax or of oil, or gazing into a polished surface, a mirror, water, or a crystal.

Omoplatoscopy (also known as **Scapulomancy**): A mantic performance by means of the shoulder-blade of a sacrificed animal heated over a fire.

Omphalomancy: Divination by the navel.

On: A magic word, used in formulae of conjurations.

Oneiroscopy: The interpretation of dreams. The magicians of ancient Egypt were skilled in inducing dreams prognosticative of the future.

Onomancy: Divination by interpreting the letters of a person's name.

Onychomancy: Divination by means of the reflections of the sun's rays.

Oöscopy: Divination by putting eggs on a fire and observing how they broke.

Ophiomancy: Divination by observation of serpents.

Ophites: An ancient Satanist society, that worshipped the constellation Ophiuchus, the Serpent-holder.

Ormuzd (another name for **Ahura Mazda**): In Zoroastrianism, the divine spirit associated with White Magic.

Ornias: A vampire-demon in the cycle of Solomonic legend. In female form, it copulates with human males.

Orniscopy: Divination by examination of bird-flight.

Ornithomancy: Synonymous with orniscopy. Divination by means of the flight of birds.

Ouanga: In Voodoo, a fetish, which may be a bone, needle, animal skin, feather.

Oupnekhat: A Sanskrit book on magic ritual, translated into Persian and, in 1802, into Latin.

Ovomancy: Divination by means of eggs. (See: Oöscopy.)

P

Pact with the Devil: To summon an evil spirit, the magician performed certain rigidly prescribed rites. One method was to cut a bough of wild hazel, that had not yet borne fruit, with a new knife, while the sun rose over the horizon. (See: New.) Carrying a bloodstone and two wax candles, the magician sought a secluded spot, such as a ruined castle or abandoned house. A triangle was traced on the floor with the bloodstone, and the candles were set at the sides of the figure. At the base of the triangle the letters I H S were written, flanked by two crosses. Around the triangle a circle was circumscribed. Standing within the triangle, and holding the hazel wand, the magician summoned the spirit with an appeal containing the following conjuration: "Aglon Tetragram Vaycheon Stimulamathon Erohares Retragsammathon Clyoran Icion Esition Existien Eryona Onera Erasyn Moyn Meffias Soter Emmanuel Saboth Adonai, I call you. Amen."

The pact involved the surrender of soul and body of the magician, at the expiration of twenty years, although, if the pact was written on virgin parchment, outside the magic circle the pact was void. Pacts were made between the magician and Satan, and written, or at least signed, in blood, the magician selling his soul and receiving from the Devil treasure, some tangible favor, or power. The formalities attending such contracts are minutely described in the Compendium Maleficarum—Witches' Manual—a seventeenth century treatise on witchcraft by Francesco Maria Guazzo.

In 1616 a witch, Stevenote de Audebert, produced in court what purported to be a contract she had made with Satan. In 1664, again, Elizabeth Style, an English witch, confessed in court to having made a pact with the Devil whereby she would have twelve years of gay and elegant life. Urbain Grandier, a magician who was executed in 1634, had made a similar pact, still preserved in the Bibliothèque Nationale, in Paris. In the library in Upsala rests another contract signed by a young undergraduate, Daniel Saltherius, who sold himself to the Devil. Saltherius later in life became a Professor of Hebrew in a German university.

Cases are recorded, however, of pledges to Satan recanted and pacts annulled. St. Basil, in the fourth century A.D., managed to retrieve a Satanic pact entered into by a young man in love with a harlot. Legend narrates that a certain Theophilus, after making a pact, repented, and recovered the contract. In the thirteenth century a Portuguese student, a certain Giles, after signing, likewise repented. He entered a monastery and one night was confronted by the Demon himself, who returned the contract in disgust.

Pamphilos: A Chaldean magician mentioned by Galen, a medical writer of the second century A.D.

Paolo Grillando: An Italian judge who published in the sixteenth century a treatise on divination, sorcery, and other occult practices.

Papaloi: A priest-magician associated with voodooism in the West Indies.

Paracelsus (circa 1490-1541): Theophrastus Bombast von Hohenheim, known as Paracelsus, was a German physician, astrologer, and magus who wandered over Europe, his methods of treatment being quite unorthodox. He was interested in occult subjects, in prognostication, and in alchemy as a means toward human perfection. He wrote on nymphs, sylphs, pigmies, and salamanders, mingling the learned results of his mystic studies with the basic folklore of his native land.

Paracelsus is known for his magic mirror, to be used in divining future events, for the making of which he gave specific directions.

Pawang: In Malaya, a beneficent magician, who helps in crop production, in locating veins of ore, and in fishing.

Pazuzu: In Babylonian demonology, the son of Hanpa, King of the Evil Spirits of the Air.

Pearls: In ancient times, pearls were believed to have occult properties and were used as amulets.

Pelesit: In Malaya, a familiar spirit. To secure a pelesit involves exhumation of the body of a first-born child.

Pentacle: A five-pointed figure used in the Middle Ages as a door sign to ward off witchcraft. In illustrations of magic apparatus in grimoires and other occult treatises, the pentacle is a design, containing magic symbols, used in divination and conjuration of spirits.

Pentagram: A five-pointed geometric figure, called the Shield of Solomon, that was used in exorcising spirits.

Pentalpha: A design formed by the interlacing of five capital A's. Used in magic rites.

Periapt: A charm or amulet. In pre-dynastic Egypt such amulets were often of green schist, inscribed with magic words of power.

Perrenon Megain: A notorious French witch who flourished in the seventeenth century.

Petchimancy: Divination by brushing clothes.

Peter of Abano (circa 1250-1310): An Italian physician born near Venice. While still young, he was initiated by a sorcerer into occult ways. Later, he traveled and studied extensively in Europe, performing many feats of wizardry. Arraigned by the Inquisition on the charge of practicing magic, he died in prison. Among his works is The Elements of Magic, or The Heptameron.

Petosiris (also called The Wheel of Beda): A device used in astrological prognostications.

Philtre: A magic potion intended to produce emotional, usually erotic, effects on the drinker. Love-philtres were well known in ancient times, and are mentioned by the Greek historian Plutarch in his Marriage Precepts.

Among the ingredients used in potions were: briony,

betel nut, frog bones, tobacco, mandrake, powdered heart of roast humming bird, sparrow liver, hare kidney, swallow womb, human blood, entrails, fingers, the heart, the genitals, excrement, the brain, flesh, hair, urine, marrow, ambergris.

In Oriental magic, love-philtres were made of the brains of a hoopee pounded into a cake, or of magic lamp wicks inscribed with invocations and then burned.

A painting by Goya depicts a witch concocting a philtre.

Phyllorhodomancy: An ancient Greek method of divination by rose-leaves.

Pico della Mirandola (1463-1494): Count Giovanni Pico della Mirandola was an Italian philosopher and mystic. His knowledge of languages included Greek, Latin, Hebrew, Chaldee, Arabic. Most of his short life was devoted to studying and writing, especially about the mystic arcana of the Kabala.

Pictorial Representations: Artists, sculptors, and etchers of the Middle Ages, the Renaissance, and as late as the eighteenth century have depicted in stone or on canvas, in prints and engravings, the characteristic features and scenes associated with witchcraft. A favorite theme was the Temptation of St. Anthony, the subject of paintings by Israel van Meckenem, the elder Brueghel, Callot, and Teniers. A witch is carved on the doorway of Lyons Cathedral. A group of four witches was depicted by both Israel van Meckenem and Albrecht Dürer. In the sixteenth century Hans Baldung portrayed witches anointing themselves for the Sabbat, while Frans Francken, in the following century, presented an assembly of witches. Goya was fascinated by the mystery of magic, and many of his subjects are drawn from this occult source. His Transformation of Sorcerers is particularly effective in its awesome implications. Each artist, in his own manner, was learned in the apparatus of wizardry, hence canvases and panels and decorative metopes abound in episodes displaying witches engaged in brewing secret potions, attendant demons in animal form, glimmering candle light against demoniac horizons, cauldrons astir with potent ingredients, warlocks immersed in grimoires.

Pierre Bonnevault: A sixteenth century French sorcerer, condemned to death for his associations with the Satanic powers.

Pietro Mora: A seventeenth century physician of Milan, who was also an alchemist, Satanist, astrologer, and wizard.

Plague: In the sixteenth century outbreaks of plague were attributed to witches in collaboration with Satan. In Geneva and other cities in Switzerland the conviction and execution of women accused of such activities reached remarkable lengths under the sponsorship of the Calvinist authorities.

Plato: Plato censures sorcerers who, for payment, are hired to practice incantations, make wax figures, and perform other magic techniques for destructive purposes.

Pliny the Elder: A Roman encyclopedist of the first century A.D. His Natural History is a rich source of information on ancient magic. He defines magic as a deceptive but powerful skill drawing elements from medicine, religion, and astrology.

Polong: In Malayan demonology, a familiar.

Poltergeist: A mischievous spirit that moves material objects, to the consternation of human beings.

Pontica: A stone with marks on it like drops of blood. It can compel demons to answer questions, and also drive them off.

Possession: A condition in which the Devil was believed to inhabit a human body. The victim experienced, among a host of physical and emotional symptoms, twitchings, biting, pinching, and burning in the stomach; the voice underwent a change, while the victim often spoke in a tongue previously unknown to him.

Priests of Sekhmet: In ancient Egypt, powerful priest-magicians.

Prophecy: Among the Egyptians, prophetic visions were believed to be induced by a preparation from hemp called assis: also by the Deadly Nightshade. In India, the seeds of Datura stramonium produced the same effects.

Pseudomonarchia Daemonum: A catalogue of sixty devils and their functions, published by Wierus in Latin in 1563.

Psychomancy: Divination by conjuring the dead, a common practice in ancient Greece.

Pythia: In ancient Greece, a priestess who acted as a mantic medium for the utterances of the oracles of the gods. While in a trance, or after drinking blood, or being overpowered by incense fumes, she made her ambivalent prophecies.

Pyromancy: Divination by means of fire.

Q

Quintus Serenus Sammonicus: A third century Roman physician who mingles magical features with medical practice.

Quirin (Quirim): A magic stone, found in lapwings' nests: also called The Traitors' Stone. When placed on the head of a sleeping person, it induces him to utter his innermost thoughts.

R

Rain: The priestesses among the Druids of ancient Gaul produced rain magically by sprinkling water over or near nude virgins.

Ralaratri: In Hindu mythology, a witch: also a vampire.

Ramirat: In Hebraic tradition, the prince of the Jinn.

Raymund Lully (1235-1315): A Spanish Kabalist and alchemist, deeply versed in Arabic. As an alchemist, he is known for the gold that he made, called after him aurum Raymundi.

Red Book of Appin: A famous grimoire.

Red cap: In Irish demonology, witches wore such caps when attending the Sabbat.

Red Dragon: A grimoire that gives directions to the karcist or adept for making magic circles and performing the other ritual requirements in invoking demons.

Reputed Magicians: In the Middle Ages manuals and other types of treatises on the occult arts acquired a heightened repute and authenticity by being attributed to men whose names had themselves acquired a legendary potency. Among such hypothetical authors were Moses, Solomon, Zoroaster, Aristotle, Alexander the Great, Vergil, St. Jerome, and Mahommed.

Restoration of virility: This practice, common among all peoples, is described by the Roman novelist Petronius in connection with the operations of an old witch: Satyricon, chapter 131.

Rhabdomancy: The art of discovering hidden objects with the aid of a rod or twig. Reference to such a rod appears in Psalms 125.3 and also in Hosea 4.12. The divining rod is still used for finding underground water and mineral ore.

Rhapsodomancy: A method of divination by opening a

poet's work at random and reading the first verse presented. (See: Stelcheomancy.)

Rhombus: Among the Greeks, a magic instrument used in drawing lots and other occult practices.

Ring of Gyges: A ring, made of mercury and inscribed with a Biblical quotation, used to confer invisibility.

Robert Fludd (1574-1637): An English Kabalist who wrote two works, Mosaical Philosophy and Summum Bonum, in which he defended magic and occult arts.

Roger Bacon (1214-1294): An English Franciscan Friar, a philosopher and scientist, whose voluminous writings emphasized the experimental approach to knowledge and who attacked traditional human delusions and superstitions. Endowed with scientific perceptiveness, he accepted what is called natural magic—that is, the phenomena within the fields of mathematics and physics; but he rejected the black arts as sinister and destructive media. He consistently challenged the fabrication of pseudo-magical and mystic apparitions, the invocation of spirits, the efficacy of charms and incantations. Yet for centuries Bacon was widely acclaimed as a magician.

Roger Bolingbroke: A notorious fifteenth century wizard, an evoker of demons, skilled in magic and astrology, who was hanged in London in the reign of Henry VI of England for attempting to kill the monarch by witchcraft.

Royal Library: The Royal Library of Rameses III of Egypt contained many books of magic that gave specific instructions on consummating the occult formulae and words of power.

S

Sabbat Broth: Made of dead children's flesh, black millet, toads, magic powders, and the flesh of a hanged man, it gave the power of flight and of prediction.

Sagana: A Roman witch mentioned by the poet Horace as an associate of the witch Canidia.

Saint-Germain: The Count of Saint-Germain was an eighteenth century Man of Mystery. He was attached to the court of Louis XV of France and moved in court circles. He claimed that he was 2000 years old and could recall in detail remote historical events. He was known to speak and write a dozen Western and Oriental languages. He had mastered alchemy and the transmutation of metals, could make himself invisible, and even corresponded, after his putative death, with the French nobility. He wrote an occult treatise entitled La Très Sainte Trinosophie, which he is said to have destroyed before his end.

Sakra El-Marid: According to Arab demonographers, a demon that was chained by King Solomon to Mount Dubavend.

Salagrama: In Hindu mythology, a stone with magic properties, worn as an amulet.

Salmon of Knowledge: Eo Feasa, in Celtic wizardry, was the Salmon of Knowledge that conferred prescience when a thumb was laid on the fish. The thumb, scalded, was then placed in the mouth of the officiant.

Salvius Julianus: A Roman Emperor of the second century A.D. who was a devotee of magic.

Sam: An Egyptian amulet, of phallic shape, used to attract erotic relationships.

Sanaves: Amulets worn by the women of Madagascar. Pieces of aromatic wood wrapped in cloth, they are suspended from the neck or the wrists, and are used as a protection against magicians.

Sasa: Also known as the shadow. In Jamaican lore, an invisible spirit of man or beast that causes evil to the living.

Satan: The most popular conception of Satan in the Middle Ages was in the form of a goat. Hence horns, hoofs, and tail were intimately linked with Satanic practices.

Satanic Names: The various names applied to the Devil have each their own etymological significance. Asmodeus, for instance, means "Creature of judgment." Satan is "Adversary." Behemoth means "Beast." Diabolus means two morsels "For he kills two things, the body and soul," declares the Malleus Maleficarum. Demon means "Cunning over blood." Diabolus, again, in its Greek etymology, would mean "Downflowing." Belial signifies "Without a master," while Beelzebub connotes "Lord of Flies."

Satanism: In the fifteenth, sixteenth, and seventeenth centuries the belief in a material Arch Fiend was so intense and prevalent throughout Europe, particularly in country districts remote from city life, that some fifty ecclesiastical and secular prohibitions were promulgated against Satanism. Hundreds of sorcerers were consequently condemned to death by burning, hanging, or, in fewer cases, to banishment.

Satan's Black Missal: A book of Satanic prayers used in the Black Mass.

Scapulomancy: A method of divination by observation of the shoulder blade of sacrificial animals, heated over a fire.

Scarab: The image of the sacred Egyptian beetle, usually made of marble, limestone, or green basalt. It symbolized the afterlife, and possessed magic potency. In magic practives it was used as a talisman.

Schemhamphoras: The mystical seventy-two divine or angelic names discussed in the Kabala.

Seal of the Snake: A stone reputedly taken from a snake's head and used as a love charm among Moslems.

Semothees: Another name for Druids.

Sena: An island off the coast of Brittany inhabited, according to the Roman geographer Pomponius Mela, by nine women, called Gallicenae, who practiced occult arts and were able to raise storms and winds and change into animal forms.

Serpent's Egg: A putative reptilian egg, small and hard, procurable only in summer in a certain phase of the moon. The Druids wore, suspended from the neck, a magic amulet called a "serpent's egg." In the form of an oval crystal ball, it was believed to have been produced by the foam resulting from the conjunction of snakes.

Set: An Egyptian evil demon.

Setnau Kha-em-Uast: An ancient Egyptian prince versed in magical lore.

Shedim: A Talmudic term for demons, who were considered to have been created by God.

Sibly: Ebenezer Sibly was an English physician who wrote a voluminous New and Complete Illustration of the Occult Sciences, in 1790, in which he confirms his belief in demons and occult forces.

Sideromancy: Divination by means of straws thrown on a hot iron.

Sihr: The Iranian term for sorcery.

Silver Bough: In Celtic Legend, a bough cut from a mystic apple tree and producing an irresistible magic melody, that served as a talisman for entrance into the Land of the Gods.

Simon Magus: A sorcerer who appears in the Acts of the Apostles, chapter 8:

> But there was a certain man, called Simon, which beforetime in the same city used sorcery, and bewitched the people of Samaria.

His master in occultism was Dositheus, and legend credited him with the power of levitation and of mass hypnotism. Simon Magus reappears in Irish folklore in association with Druidic practices, becoming known as Simon the Druid.

Sir Francis Dashwood: An eighteenth century occultist, Superior of the secret, obscene Satanic circle known as the Medmenham Franciscans.

Solomon: A large body of apocryphal tales, during more than two thousand years, has grown up around the personality and accomplishments of this unique king. He has become a mystical, universal figure, appearing in both Oriental and Western literature, folklore, and legends, many of which dwell on the occult powers of the monarch. An Abyssinian legend relates that Solomon, once seized by demon blacksmiths, saved himself by thrice repeating the magical term: Lofaham.

On another occasion, when the king of the demons sent his minions to take out the hearts of men, Solomon thrice repeated the spell:

> Lofaham,
> Solomon,
> Iyouel,
> Iyosenaoui.

Solomon is credited among other activities with having written many books on magic, among them The Key of Solomon, explaining methods of summoning and mastering the demons. In his Antiquities of the Jews the historian Josephus refers to Solomon's skill in this respect. In all his dealings, in fact, the king enlisted the aid of the spirits: in using the magic carpet that transported himself and his armies through the air, and in the building of the Temple with the aid of demons.

Solomon's Lamp: A lamp in the possession of King Solomon, by means of which he could command the spirits of hell. Aladdin's lamp, that appears in the cycle of Arab folktales, is of a similar type.

Solomon's Mirror: A polished plate used in magic ceremonies.

Solomon's Ring: A ring studded with stones that had magic properties and gave King Solomon dominion over the world of spirits.

Sons of Cham-Zoroaster: The four sons of Cham-Zoroaster: Cush, Mizraim, Phut, and Canaan were lords of magic over their respective territories—Africa, Egypt, the desert tribes, and Phoenicia.

Sorcerer: An adept in occult practices, bound to Satan in return for knowledge and skill in the magic arts. He is usually represented as having a fixed stare, while his power remains intact provided his feet are in contact with the ground.

Sortilege: Divination by lots. This technique includes rhabdomancy, belomancy, and similar procedures.

Spatulamancy: In Scotland, this is called divination by Speal Bone, i.e., the blade bone of a shoulder of mutton.

Spell: A spoken or written formula, or a symbol, used to produce magical effects.

Sphondulomancy: Divination by means of spindles.

Spider: A baked spider was often worn as an amulet against witchcraft.

Spitting: When renouncing the Devil, a sorcerer spat thrice, an act that released him from demoniac power.

Spudomancy: Divination by means of cinders from sacrificial fires.

Srei ap: In Cambodian demonology, ghouls.

Stichomancy: Divination by opening a book at random and interpreting the first words read.

Stolcheomancy: A method of divination by opening a poet's work at random and reading the first verse presented. (See: Rhapsodomancy.)

Stolisomancy: An ancient method of divination by observing a person's manner of dressing.

Stone of Knellar: A stone, in Aberdeenshire, Scotland, that has inscribed on it Druidic magic symbols.

Succubus: A female demon that copulated with human males. The princess of all the succubi was called Nahemah.

Sukias: In Central American demonology, witches.

Swawmx: In Burmese demonology, vampires.

Swords: Witches' swords, used in magic operations, were

made according to the prescriptions in the Key of Solomon, with Hebrew Kabalistic inscriptions on the hilt and blade.

Sword of Moses: A tenth century A.D. treatise that contains magic prescriptions and formulas for counteracting human ills.

Sworn Book of Honorius: A fourteenth century work on magic.

T

Taboos: Magic taboos and prohibitions, called geas, are frequent in Gaelic legend. The taboo is the result of a spell cast, by means of rhythmic enchantment, by a wizard's will power. One such spell, known as fith-fath, produced invisibility and transformation from human to animal shape. The belief in such spells still lingers in some remote Hebridean Islands.

Tadibe: A Siberian magician.

Taghairm: In Celtic demonology, a method of divination by evocation of spirits. The seer, wrapped in the hide of a newly-slaughtered bull, awaited the spirits near a waterfall or a precipice.

A taghairm was also the name given to a sacrifice of cats to the infernal powers. One of the last taghairms of this kind was held in the middle of the seventeenth century, on the island of Mull, in the Scottish Hebrides.

Talisman: (See: Amulet.)

Tarni: Formulae of exorcism employed by the Kalmuks. Written on parchment and hung on a sick person's neck, the talisman had an apotropaic effect.

Tarot: A series of seventy-eight playing cards, decorated with fantastic and mystic diagrams and symbols, used in divination.

Tchatcha-em-ankh: An Egyptian priest-magician, of the fourth millennium B.C., who by magic incantation raised the waters of a lake.

Tempting powder: In Jamaican Obeah, a love potion.

Temura: A Kabalistic method, by permutations and combinations, of decoding the cipher significances in the Old Testament.

Tephromancy: Divination by writing in ashes.

Teraphim: Among the ancient Syrians, household gods or

85

idols that uttered oracular truth. They were also used among the Israelites.

Testament of Solomon: In autobiographical form, a treatise, based on Old Testament sources, that describes the magic powers of King Solomon and his construction of the Temple with the aid of demons. It contains detailed descriptions and names and functions of demoniac beings and their astounding prophecies.

Teta: An ancient Egyptian thaumaturgist of the fourth millennium B.C.

Tetragrammaton: The most effective word in magic performances was the Tetragrammaton, the Kabalistic term for the four-letter name of God. This term involved mystic combinations of letters and of attributes having multi-lettered names, some consisting of as many as seventy-two elements.

Tezcatlipoca: An ancient Mexican devil-deity, god of hell. Also known as Yaotzin, The Enemy. He was the object of worship of the Mexican witches at their Sabbat.

Thaumaturgy: The practice of "working wonders": witchcraft, magic.

Theodoris of Lemnos: An ancient Greek witch, mentioned by the orator Demosthenes, in the fourth century B.C., as having been condemned to death for her enchantments. Herodotus the historian declares that Lemnos had a reputation for sorcery.

Thessaly: A district of northern Greece, famous in ancient times for its witchcraft. Magicians, necromancers, and all adepts in the black arts were considered either as having come from Thessaly or as having been trained there. The Greek dramatist Sophocles and the comic writer Menander refer to the powers of Thessalian magicians. Among the Romans, the poets Vergil, Ovid, and Lucan describe Thessaly as the source of witchcraft. In the second century A.D. Apuleius, himself reputedly a sorcerer, produced a fantastic novel—Metamorphoses or The Golden Ass—packed with scenes of magic and strange transformations.

Thöck: An ancient Nordic witch.

Thoth: An ancient Egyptian god of magic: also the inventor of language.

Thrace: A district of Greece that, like Thessaly, was notorious for witchcraft.

Thumb of Knowledge: An occult gesture, consisting of pressure on a tooth with the thumb, made by the Celtic sorcerer intent on achieving supernatural vision.

Thundering Rod: The sorcerer's magic wand.

Thursday: This day was sacred to the witches attending the Sabbat.

Among the Iranians, the spirits of the dead were believed to be free on Thursday to revisit their terrestrial homes.

Tii: In Polynesian demonology, a vampire.

Tiromancy: An obscure method of divination by means of cheese.

Toad: In magic symbolism, the toad was considered a venomous reptile. It was used in the Sabbat ritual.

Tomga: An Eskimo familiar.

Tonalamatl: An ancient Mexican Book of Fate, containing magic prescriptions and rituals for appeasing demons.

Tower of the Witches: A tower at Lindheim, Germany, that, in the Middle Ages, was a rendezvous for witches bent on conjuring demons.

Trial by ordeal: A mediaeval method of testing the authenticity of facts, the innocence of an accused person, the validity of an oath, or the thaumaturgic capacity of a reputed witch, by exposing the person involved to certain ordeals. These ordeals included walking through fire, trial by blood, trial by combat, ordeal by water, by poison or by torture. The belief was that the innocent would emerge unharmed from such an ordeal. Whoever succumbed to the test was thus assumed guilty. Hence whoever was accused of witchcraft was, by these tests, demonstrably a witch or a sorcerer.

Triskelion: A symbol consisting of three legs bent at the knee and joined at the thigh, used as a charm against the

Evil Eye. The figure is found on ancient Mediterranean coins of the fifth century B.C.

Trithemius (1462-1516): John Trithemius was a German abbot of Würzburg, a friend of Agrippa von Nettesheim. Trithemius was a prominent scholar, and wrote on magic and alchemy. There was a legend that he exorcised the dead Mary of Burgundy, wife of the Emperor Maximilian. Hesitant about the possible punishment as a result of publishing works on magic, he wrote in Latin in symbolic language, recognizable to initiates only.

Tuathy De Danann: In Irish legend, ancient underground gods, the people of the goddess Danu, who were magicians, skilled in runes and spells.

Tunisa: In Burmese demonology, seers, diviners.

Turifumy: Divination by incense smoke.

Tututash: In Iranian demonology, a sorcerer, king of the Jewish djinn.

Two-tailed lizard: A magic papyrus prescribes:
> Put a two-tailed lizard into oil and cook it, and anoint the man with it, and then he dies.

U

Ushabti: In ancient Egypt, a symbolic figurine entombed along with the dead.

Usurtu: In Chaldean demonology, a kind of protective wall against demoniac malevolence, made by sprinkling lime and flour. This corresponds to the magic circle.

Utchat: An Egyptian name for the amulet that is also called The Eye of Horus.

Uther Pendragon: A wizard who appears in Welsh legend.

V

Valentine Graterakes: An Irish physician of the seventeenth century who performed cures by occult means. Many of his remarkable cures were achieved by "touch."

Vampire: A ghost or sometimes a human being that sucks human blood. Vampires are associated chiefly, but not exclusively, with European folklore. In Slavic countries it was believed that a child born with a tooth would become a vampire. In Poland vampires were called Upirs. In Greece they are still known as Brucolacas.

Velleda: A priestess-diviner of ancient Gaul and Germany, mentioned by the Roman historian Tacitus.

Vercan: A powerful demon, invoked in conjurations.

Verdelet: A demon who is in charge of transporting witches to the Sabbat.

Vervain: The plant verbena: used as an ingredient in witches' ointment. It was believed to render them invisible.

Viedma: A Russian term for a witch.

Vikodlak: A Slavonic term for a vampire.

Voodoo (Voodooism): The practice of magic rites prevalent in the West Indies, particularly Haiti.

Originally stemming from ophiolatry transmitted from African Ashanti cults, voodoo is characterized by erotic and symbolic dance rhythms, accompanied by corresponding drum tattoos. Occult chants, sacrifices of chickens and goats are other features of voodoo ritual. Voodoo is still practiced in remote regions of Haiti. As late as the first decades of this century it involved ophiolatry, human sacrifice, and anthropophagism.

W

Walking: Walking left-handwise, or "against the sun," was characteristic of practitioners of black magic.

Wanga: In Haiti, magic. It also implies, as magic often does, empirical medicine.

Warlock: A magician or male witch.

Washing-woman: In Celtic demonology, a spirit of a woman, washing a shroud, seen after nightfall. Meeting her presages death.

Weather: In Malayan magic, incantations are used to control weather conditions; to summon a wind, allay a storm, or bring rain.

Werewolf: A person who can change himself into a wolf. The Roman novelist Petronius tells a remarkable werewolf story in the Banquet of Trimalchio. (See: Lycanthropy.)

Wierus (1516-1588): Wierus, whose original name was John Weyer, was a pupil of Agrippa. He wrote De Praestigiis Daemonum et incantationibus ac veneficiis—on the activities of demons, incantations, and sorceries.

William Beckford: The eighteenth century author of Vathek, who also dabbled in Oriental magic, Kabalistic lore, and demonology in general.

Witch: This expression, now denoting a female magician, derives from Old English wicca, a man who practices magic. In the Middle Ages the term witch was of common gender.

According to the Malleus Maleficarum, one of the most important treatises on witchcraft, witches were anthropophagists. They were capable of raising hailstorms, causing sterility in man and beast. They consorted carnally with demons, and their offspring were equally demoniac. They could transport themselves at will, strike an enemy with lightning, influence court decrees, bewitch by mere look, and cause calamities and death.

Witch Mountains: Certain mountains in Europe were closely associated with witches' gatherings. In Carpathia there was the Babia Gora—The Old Women's Mountain. In Germany, there were a number of such mountains, in Thuringia, Westphalia, and elsewhere: The Huiberg, near Halberstadt, the Horselberg, the Köterberg, the Staffelstein.

In France, there was the Puy de Dôme. In Italy: Barco di Ferrara, Paterno di Bologna, Spirato della Mirandola, Tossale di Bergamo.

Witches' Butter: In Swedish legend, cats, the familiars of witches, were so well fed that while accompanying their mistresses on a Sabbat assembly they often vomited on to kitchen gardens. The result was called Witches' Butter.

Witches' Circle: A circle intended to keep within its area the occult power aroused by the witches.

Witches' Sabbat: An assembly of witches and magicians, held every three months: on February 2nd, Walpurgis Night, which was May Day Eve, on Midsummer Eve, and on November Eve. The witches, anointing themselves with the fat of children slain or exhumed from graves, or using belladonna and aconite as "flying ointments," came riding through the air on goats, distaffs, rakes, broomsticks, and even in carriages. They had an opportunity of meeting the Devil himself at such gatherings, which took place on a mountain top or at a crossroads. Usually, a dead tree stood nearby, or a gibbet.

Satan himself presided, in the form of a raven, a cat, or a goat, or even in human form. Initial homage was paid by the assembled witches to the Grand Master with the osculum infame, a kiss on the posteriors. As their own contribution, witches brought stolen or their own children as neophytes in the service of Satan.

Occasionally, at these gatherings, the witches stripped naked, as is evident from many mediaeval paintings and woodcuts.

Men and women of "quality," courtiers, landed gentlemen, wealthy and distinguished also participated in the Sabbat, as mediaeval paintings of witch scenes indicate.

Witches' Unguent: A venomous concoction, compounded of toad, cat, lizard, and vipers, used by witches in poisoning crops.

Witch-hunting: This practice, of searching out suspected witches, torturing them to the point of confession, and condemning them to death after a perfunctory trial, was sporadic throughout the Middle Ages. But it reached a greater intensity, sponsored by religious and civic bodies, in the sixteenth and seventeenth centuries, which were marked by numberless mass witch burnings. Such operations occurred especially in France, Germany, Italy, Spain, and Denmark. In England, Lancashire was the locale of many investigations, trials and convictions, on varying degrees of hearsay and subjective evidence, of women accused of witchcraft. Similar campaigns were carried out late in the same century in southern England; while in the United States the Salem witch-hunts of New England became notorious for the ruthlessness of their prosecution.

Witchcraft and Papists: In seventeenth century England and in Switzerland witch-hunting was closely associated with the persecution of Roman Catholics. Catholicism, in fact, and witchcraft were, in a political sense and religious sense, considered synonymous, according to contemporary historical and parliamentary records, pamphlets, diaries, biographies, state trials, and memoirs.

Witchcraft in Rome: The ancient Romans had knowledge of the cap of invisibility and of the divining rod. In the century before Christ King Mithridates of Pontus in Asia Minor introduced many Oriental branches of magic into Rome.

The Roman novelist Petronius mentions the term succubus, but probably with the meaning of a changeling. So Apuleius calls Psyche a succuba. Apuleius, again, in the same Metamorphoses, describes how two witches cut out the heart of a faithless lover and replaced it with a sponge.

The historian Tacitus mentions the rites of magicians and Chaldeans, and alludes to the significant part played by these wizards and diviners in the interpretation of dreams and administering philtres. According to Tacitus, they were implicated in political unrest, in sudden, unaccountable deaths, and in criminal trials.

Wizards: In the reign of Charles IX of France, it is estimated that some 30,000 sorcerers lived in Paris alone, while the rest of France contained another 100,000.

Writers on witchcraft: By a not unexpected association, many writers on magic have been priests and ecclesiastics: for religion and magic have from the most remote times been intimately linked. Among such writers are Martin Delrio, Kramer and Sprenger, Guazzo, Sinistrari, Cotton Mather, and, in contemporary times, the Rev. Montague Summers and Father J. J. Williams.

X

Xylomancy: Divination by observing the position of twigs lying on the ground.

Y

Yatu: In Zoroastrianism, a sorcerer.

Y-Kim: An ancient, obscure Chinese book, attributed to the fourth millennium B.C., dealing with Kabalistic mysticism. The Key to this work is called the Trigrams of Fo-Hi, after the name of the Emperor Fo-Hi, the putative author.

Z

Zabulon: A demon.

Zapan: A demon who officiates in the Infernal Regions.

Zardhust: Also called Zoroaster. An ancient magician who came from China.

Zekerboni: A famous seventeenth century grimoire, written by Pietro Mora and full of detailed prescriptions for incantations, spells, charms, and especially conjurations.

Zlata Ulicka: The Street of Gold. A famous mediaeval street in Prague that was the haunt of alchemists and the location of their laboratories.

Zlito: A fourteenth century sorcerer, famous at the court of Wenceslaus of Bohemia.

Zlokobinca: A Slavonic term for a witch.

Zombie: A term associated with Haitian voodoo. A zombie is a human being whose soul has been extracted by a magician. The body is dug up after burial and given a semblance of life. The zombie can participate in ordinary human activities, but under certain conditions it is forced to return to its grave.

Selective Bibliography

The bibliography on witchcraft, ranging over every continent and covering more than three thousand years, is so vast and multifarious in its impacts on religious, political, social, and literary areas that only a fraction of the most significant works can be listed. There are bibliographical compilations, each embracing thousands of items, on the subject, that fill American and European libraries.

A famous collection of books on magic is housed in the Library of Congress, Washington, D. C. It was the gift of Harry Houdini. Another collection, reaching some 12,000 volumes, is owned by Dr. O. R. Schlag, of Zurich, Switzerland.

W. H. D. Adams. Witch, warlock and magician. London, 1889.

Johannes Laurentius Anania. De Natura Daemonum. Venice, 1581.

John Ashton. The Devil in Britain and America. London, 1896.

Francis Barrett. The Magus. 3 vols. London, 1801.

Hesketh J. Bell. Obeah. London, 1889.

Jean Bodin. De la Démonomanie des sorciers. Paris, 1580.

Henri Boguet. Discours des sorciers. Lyons, 1608.

Jules Bois. Le Satanisme. Paris, 1890.

Alexandre Bonneau. Haiti—ses progrès—son avenir. Paris, 1862.

Richard Boulton. Complete History of magic, sorcery, and witchcraft. London, 1715.

E. A. Wallis Budge. Egyptian Magic. London, 1899.

J. G. Campbell. Witchcraft and second sight in the Highlands and Islands of Scotland. MacLehose. Glasgow, 1902.

Paul Carus. History of the Devil and the idea of Evil. Open Court Publishing Company. Chicago, 1900.

G. Contenau. La magie chez les Assyriens et les Babyloniens. Payot, Paris, 1947.

Thomas Cooper. The mystery of witchcraft. 1617.

Alasteir Crowley. Magick in theory and practice. Lecram Press. Paris, 1929.

Lambertus Danaeus. De Veneficiis. Cologne, 1575.

Antoine-Louis Daugis. Traité de la Magie. 1732.

Hassoldt David. Sorcerers' Village. Little, Brown. New York, 1955.

Alexandra David-Neel. With mystics and magicians in Tibet. Lane. London, 1934.

Alexandra David-Neel. Magic and mystery in Tibet. Crown. New York, 1937.

T. W. Davies. Magic, divination and demonology among the Hebrews and their neighbors. London, 1898.

L. Decle. Three Years in Savage Africa. Methuen. London, 1898.

Martin Delrio. Disquisitionum Magicarum Libri Sex. Louvain, 1599.

Albrecht Dieterich. Abraxas. Leipzig, 1891.

P. L. Elich. Daemonomagia. Frankfort, 1607.

F. T. Elworthy. The Evil Eye. London, 1895.

Joseph Ennemoser. History of Magic. English translation. 2 vols. London, 1854.

C. H. L'Estrange Ewen. Witchcraft and demonianism. Heath Cranston. London, 1933.

J. S. Fairfax. Demonologia. 1827.

C. Fossey. La magie assyrienne. Paris, 1902.

J. G. Frazer. Magic art and the evolution of kings. 2 vols. Macmillan. London, 1917.

J. G. Frazer. Folklore in the Old Testament. 3 vols. Macmillan. London, 1919.

J. C. Frommann. De Fascinatione. Nuremberg, 1674.

Moses Gaster. The Sword of Moses. London, 1896.

Moses Gaster. Studies and texts in magic, mediaeval romance, Hebrew apocrypha and Samaritan archaeology. 3 vols. Maggs Bros. London, 1925-1928.

Lazare de Gérin-Ricard. Histoire de l'occultisme. Payot. Paris, 1947.

Mathieu Giraldo. Histoire curieuse et pittoresque des sorciers. 1846.

Rupert Gleadow. Magic and Divination. Faber. London, 1941.

William Godwin. Lives of the Necromancers. F. J. Mason. London, 1834.

J. B. Gouriet. Les charlatans célèbres. 2 vols. Lerouge. Paris, 1819.

M. Graubard. Astrology and alchemy. Philosophical Library. New York, 1953.

Francesco Guazzo. Compendium Maleficarum. Milan, 1608.

Franz Hartmann. Magic white and black. Eckler. New York, 1910.

H. Hay, editor. Cyclopedia of Magic. McKay. New York, 1949.

V. Henry. La magie dans l'Inde antique. Dujarric. Paris, 1904.

Wilhelm Hertz. Der Werwolf. Stuttgart, 1862.

Christine Hole. Witchcraft in England. Batsford. London, 1945.

M. O. Howey. The Horse in magic and myth. Rider. London, 1923.

Pennethorne Hughes. Witchcraft. Longmans. London, 1952.

Zora Neale Hurston. Voodoo gods. Dent. London, 1939.

F. Hutchinson. Essay concerning witchcraft. London, 1718.

Iamblichus. The mysteries of the Egyptians, Chaldeans and Assyrians. Translated by Taylor. Chiswick, 1821.

B. Jacob. Im Namen Gottes. Calvary and Co. Berlin, 1903.

King James I. Daemonologie. 1599.

F. Kaigh. Witchcraft and magic of Africa. Lesley. London, 1947.

Leonard W. King. Babylonian magic and sorcery. London, 1896.

George Lyman Kittredge. Witchcraft in Old and New England. Harvard University Press. Cambridge, 1929.

Lacnunga. Anglo-Saxon magic and medicine. Edited by J. H. G. Grattan and C. Singer. Oxford University Press, 1952.

Pierre de L'Ancre. L'Incrédulité et mescréance du sortilège. Paris, 1622.

E. Laurent. Magica Sexualis. Privately printed for the Anthropological Press. New York, 1934.

Henry Charles Lea. Materials toward a history of witchcraft. 3 vols. University of Pennsylvania Press. Philadelphia, 1939.

François Lenormant. La magie des Chaldéens. Paris, 1874.

Marc Leproux. Médicine, magie et sorcellerie. Presses Universitaires de France. Paris, 1955.

Eliphas Lévi. History of Magic. Translated by A. E. Waite. Rider. London, 1913.

J. A. Lowe. Magic in Greek and Latin literature. Blackwell. Oxford, 1929.

Charles Mackay. Strange Movements. London, 1869.

M. Magre. Magicians, seers and mystics. Translated from the French. Dutton and Company. New York, 1932.

J. Mason. Anatomie of Sorcery. 1612.

S. L. M. Mathers, editor. The Key of Solomon the King. Redway, 1889.

S. L. M. Mathers, editor. The Book of sacred magic of Abramelin the sage. 1898.

F. A. Maury. La magie et l'astrologie dans l'antiquité et du moyen âge. 4th edition. Didier. Paris, 1877.

J. Michelet. La sorcière. Paris, 1862.

Ulrich Molitor. De lamiis et phitonicis muliebribus. Constance, 1489.

J. A. Montgomery. Aramaic incantation text from Nippur.

University of Pennsylvania Museum. Philadelphia, 1913.

Henri Roger Gougenot des Mousseaux. Remarkable Phenomena of magic. 1864.

Margaret Alice Murray. The witch-cult in Western Europe. Clarendon Press. 1921.

Gérard de Nerval. Les Alluminés. Paris, 1841.

A. D. Nock. Greek magic papyri. (In Journal of Egyptian Archaeology. vol. 15. London, 1929.)

Wallace Notestein. History of English witchcraft. American Historical Association. Washington, 1910.

J. L. Pitts. Witchcraft and devil lore in the Channel Islands. Guernsey, 1886.

Jacques Collin de Plancy. Dictionnaire infernal. 4 vols. Definitive edition. Plon. Paris, 1863.

E. Radford. Encyclopedia of superstitions. Philosophical Library. New York, 1949.

Nicholas Rémy. Demonolatria. Lyons, 1595.

H. T. F. Rhodes. The Satanic Mass. Rider. London, 1954.

A. Ricardus. De praestigiis et incantationibus daemonum. Basel, 1568.

Viktor Rydberg. The magic of the Middle Ages. Holt. New York, 1879.

E. Salverte. Des sciences occultes. Paris, 1843.

Reginald Scot. The Discovery of Witchcraft. 1665.

C. K. Sharpe. Witchcraft. Historical account of the belief in witchcraft in Scotland. London, 1881.

Ludovico Maria d'Ameno Sinistrari. De la démonalité et des animaux incubes et succubes. Translated into French. Paris, 1876.

W. M. Skeat. Malay Magic. Macmillan. London, 1900.

W. G. Soldan and U. Hepper. Geschichte der Hexenprozesse. Munich, 1912.

Lewis Spence. Encyclopedia of Occultism. Routledge. London, 1920.

B. H. Springett. Secret sects of Syria and Lebanon. Allen and Unwin. London, 1922.

G. Storms. Anglo-Saxon Magic. Nijhoff. The Hague, 1948.

Christian Stridtbeckh. On Witches. Academic dissertation. Leipzig, 1690.

M. Summers. History of witchcraft and demonology. Knopf. New York, 1926.

M. Summers. Geography of witchcraft. Knopf. New York, 1927.

Tartarotti. Del congresso notturno delle Lamie libri tre. 1749.

E. Tavenner. Studies in magic from Latin literature. Columbia University Press. New York, 1916.

C. J. S. Thompson. Mystery and secrets of magic. Lippincott. Philadelphia, 1928.

Lynn Thorndike. History of magic and experimental science. Six volumes. Columbia University Press. New York, 1923-1941.

Auguste Viatte. Victor Hugo et les illuminés de son temps. Editions de l'arbre. Montreal, 1942.

A. E. Waite. The mysteries of magic. 2nd edition. London, 1897.

A. E. Waite. The book of black magic and of pacts. London, 1898.

J. W. Wickwar. Witchcraft and the black art. McBride. New York, 1926.

Charles Williams. Witchcraft. Faber. London, 1941.

Joseph J. Williams, S.J. Voodoohs and Obeahs. Dial Press. New York, 1932.

R. Winstedt. Malay magician. Revised. Routledge. London, 1954.

T. Wright. Narratives of sorcery and magic. 2 vols. R. Bentley. London, 1851.

Acknowledgments

The author wishes to make due acknowledgments in the following cases for the use of some factual and illustrative material:

Bruno de Jésus-Marie, editor. Satan. Sheed and Ward. New York, 1952.

E. M. Butler. Ritual Magic. Cambridge University Press, 1949.

R. T. Davis. Four Centuries of Witch Beliefs. Methuen. London, 1947.

Vergilius Ferm, editor. Dictionary of Religion. Philosophical Library. New York, 1945.

R. F. Fortune. Sorcerers of Dobu. Dutton and Co. New York, 1932.

Gerald B. Gardner. Witchcraft Today. Rider. London, 1954.

Frank Gaynor. Dictionary of Mysticism. Philosophical Library. New York, 1953.

Grillot de Givry. Witchcraft, Magic and Alchemy. George Harrap and Co. London, 1931.

Eliphas Lévi. History of Magic. Rider. London, 1913.

Margaret Alice Murray. The God of the Witches. Oxford University Press. New York, 1952.

H. T. F. Rhodes. The Satanic Mass. Rider. London, 1954.

P. W. Sergeant. Witches and Warlocks. Hutchinson. London, 1936.

Kurt Seligmann. History of Magic. Pantheon Books. New York, 1948.

St. John D. Seymour. Tales of King Solomon. Oxford University Press, 1924.

Lewis Spence. Magic Arts in Celtic Britain. Rider. London, 1945.

Lewis Spence. History and Origins of Druidism. Rider. London, n.d.

Alfred Still. Borderland of Science. Philosophical Library. New York, 1950.

Montague Summers. Witchcraft and Black Magic. Rider. London, 1945.

R. C. Thompson. Semitic Magic. Luzac and Co. London, 1908.

Joseph Trachtenberg. Jewish Magic and Superstition. Behrman House. New York, 1939.